30-minute Italian

30-minute Italian

Fran Warde

Photography by David Loftus

Bounty
BOOKS

First published in Great Britain in 1998 by Hamlyn,
a division of Octopus Publishing Group Ltd.
This Revised edition first published 2004

This edition published 2005 by Bounty Books,
a division of Octopus Publishing Group Ltd
2–4 Heron Quays, London E14 4JP
Reprinted 2006
Copyright © Octopus Publishing Group Ltd 2004

ISBN-13: 978-0-753712-60-3
ISBN-10: 0-753712-60-1

A CIP catalogue record for this book is available
from the British Library

Printed and bound in China

NOTES

1 The Department of Health advises that eggs
should not be consumed raw. It is prudent for
more vulnerable people such as pregnant and
nursing mothers, invalids, the elderly, babies
and young children to avoid uncooked or lightly
cooked dishes made with eggs.

2 Meat and poultry should be cooked
thoroughly. To test if poultry is cooked, pierce
the flesh through the thickest part with a
skewer or fork – the juices should run clear,
never pink or red.

3 This book includes dishes made with nuts
and nut derivatives. It is advisable for those
with known allergic reactions to nuts and nut
derivatives and those who may be potentially
vulnerable to these allergies, such as pregnant
and nursing mothers, invalids, the elderly,
babies and children, to avoid dishes made with
nuts and nut oils. It is also prudent to check the
labels of pre-prepared ingredients for the
possible inclusion of nut derivatives.

contents

introduction

Cooking for me started at a very young age when I would help my mum in the kitchen (I'm not sure if it was help, but it was always great fun), spilling sugar and flour everywhere and seeing who could mix the fastest! As soon as she taught me that part of cooking was also clearing up, I was allowed to cook more and more – cakes on Saturday afternoon, then, later, fish pies and lasagne. I went to a boarding school with dreadful food, but on Tuesdays it was domestic science; I would try to make a decent meal for a few friends to enjoy. Everyone relied on it working out, which it generally did.

I think that these early days played a great part in creating the foundations for my cooking career. I still enjoy it and continue to learn; it's a never-ending creative process of combining colours, flavours and textures to produce a delicious meal to enjoy with friends.

I have aimed to produce imaginative and tasty recipes that are quick and simple to make (and good for you, too). The recipes in this book have been designed to show that it's possible to produce delicious, mouthwatering meals in 30 minutes – the same length of time that it takes to heat up many ready-made meals – or even less time, without resorting to convenience food.

Italian recipes fit the bill perfectly when you need good, quick meals in a hurry, for the Italians are very keen on fresh food and speedy methods of preparation. They take their food very seriously, combining a deep respect for top-quality ingredients with a great love of home cooking – in fact, the way to enjoy Italian food at its best is to eat in people's homes.

Italian food, in all its rich, regional diversity, doesn't just taste delicious – it's actually good for you, too. The Mediterranean diet, with its emphasis on fresh vegetables and fruit, fresh fish and seafood, pasta and olive oil, is reckoned to be one of the healthiest in the world, full of vitamins and minerals and low in saturated fat.

In this book I have included a lot of vegetable recipes, which work very well as supper dishes on their own. Serve two or three vegetable, pasta or rice dishes together, enjoy their delicate flavours and see how satisfied you are after the meal without feeling at all heavy or as if you have eaten too much. There are some delicious meat and fish recipes, too, which can be cooked in 30 minutes – a joy to any busy cook who doesn't want to be chained to the stove when the sun is shining outside or after a busy day at work or with the children. There are also some puddings for those special days.

I have to say that I am especially proud of the chocolate risotto, which is a totally new idea and easy to make from ingredients that can be found in any well-stocked kitchen.

Do follow the Italian example and shop carefully, though. Some of the cheaper products in our shops and supermarkets are very poor substitutes for the real thing. Never, for example, buy ready-grated Parmesan cheese; instead, buy a piece and grate it as required. A guide to the most important or unusual ingredients used in the recipes appears in the glossary that follows.

Fran Warde

glossary

balsamic vinegar This aristocrat of vinegars is made in Modena. The grape juice is aged in wooden barrels for an average of seven years. Like a good wine, balsamic vinegar needs time to mature, and the longer it is in the barrel, the deeper and sweeter the flavour.

capers Used to flavour sauces, these are the pungent, sharp-tasting buds of a shrub found in Mediterranean countries. Capers are usually bottled in brine and need to be rinsed in water before using. Small ones are the best.

cavolo nero A long, slim cabbage with a distinct sweet flavour; it is a beautiful green with a hint of purplish black.

cheeses
Dolcelatte A soft, creamy cows' milk cheese with blue veins, aged for two months; it is similar to Gorgonzola but milder.
Fontina A soft cows' milk cheese from the Val d'Aosta in the Italian Alps, which is aged for up to five months. It is reminiscent of Gruyère and used in cooking and as a dessert cheese.
Mascarpone A soft, creamy cheese made with cows' milk and used for both sweet and savoury dishes.
Mozzarella Originally made from buffaloes' milk, it is now more often made from cows' milk or a mixture of the two. Cows' milk mozzarella does not have the same softness of flavour. Mozzarella should be eaten fresh; it melts well and is frequently used on pizzas.
Parmesan This strong, hard cheese is made from partially skimmed cows' milk and aged for up to two years. The best Parmesan has the words Parmigiano-Reggiano punched into the rind. Buy it in a block and grate it as you need it.

Pecorino This ewes' milk cheese can be soft or hard depending on its age; it is made all over Italy, so flavours can vary greatly. Mature, hard pecorino is used for grating like Parmesan.
Ricotta A bland, soft, fresh cheese used as a base in fillings and frequently combined with spinach. It should be used when it is very fresh.

chocolate Bars of chocolate vary so much in their cocoa content. Look on the back of the packet and only use ones that contain at least 70% cocoa solids. I prefer Valrhona which can be found in good delicatessens.

ciabatta A popular Italian bread baked into a flat loaf with a distinctive open texture. It can have a range of flavourings added.

fennel A beautiful, fragrant vegetable with a delicate aniseed flavour, fennel is wonderful with fish; use the feathery fronds to add to salsa verde.

focaccia A flat yeast bread made with olive oil and baked in an oiled pan. It is often flavoured with garlic, herbs, sun-dried tomatoes or olives.

garlic A pungent herb used extensively in Italian cooking. Crush heavily with the side of a knife to remove the papery skin, then the clove can be chopped.

herbs

Basil The best-known Italian herb with soft, bright green leaves, basil is a vital ingredient in pesto and goes well with tomatoes. There is also a red basil with small, purplish leaves and a more delicate flavour.

Bay leaves Usually used dried in soups and stews as part of a bouquet garni.

Oregano A sweet, spicy and aromatic herb, similar to marjoram.

Rosemary Its long, spiky leaves give rosemary a distinctive appearance. It is used a great deal in Italy, particularly with chicken and lamb. Rosemary is very pungent, so should be used in moderation.

olive oil
Extra virgin olive oil, virgin olive oil and olive oil. These names refer to the way that the oil is extracted and this can greatly alter the flavour. Try to buy extra virgin oil from the first cold pressing as this will be rich in flavour and is most suitable for dressings, sauces and pouring over pasta. A less expensive oil can be used for frying.

olives
Small, oval tree fruits which ripen from green to black. For the best flavour, buy them from delicatessens that sell them loose rather than in bottles or cans.

pancetta
The same cut as streaky bacon but differently cured, pancetta is found in supermarkets or in delicatessens. It is also sold as pancetta arrotolata, in a roll like salami. Buy a 1 cm/½ inch slice, unroll it and use as pancetta.

panettone
A baked yeast cake from Milan enriched with egg yolks, raisins and candied peel. Panettone is traditionally served at Christmas or with coffee; it is very good toasted at breakfast.

parma ham
A great Italian delicacy, this cured ham comes from the area around Parma in the Emilia-Romagna region of northern Italy. The skin is rubbed in salt, then the hams are hung in cellars to mature for 8–10 months. Parma ham must be served thinly sliced; it is eaten on its own or with melon or fresh figs.

pasta
This is made from hard durum wheat flour and water. If it is made with eggs, it is called *pasta all'ouvo*. I prefer fresh pasta but a good dried Italian brand can be substituted. The Italians do not usually eat pasta as a main course, but serve a light pasta dish between the antipasti and the main course. It is available in a bewildering range of shapes and sizes.

pasta shapes

Farfalle or **farfallini** Pasta bows.

Fusilli Pasta twists or corkscrews.

Lasagne Large sheets of pasta used for baked dishes. Sheets can be cut to fit cooking dishes.

Linguine Long, thin, flat ribbon noodles.

Pappardelle Wide pasta noodles.

Penne Sometimes known as quills, these are short, tubular lengths of pasta.

Orecchiette Small, round, ear-shaped pasta.

Orzo A very small pasta shape, which looks rather like grains of rice.

Spaghetti Long, string-like pasta.

Tagliatelle Long, flat ribbon noodles.

Tortellini Pasta twists with various fillings.

pine nuts Small, slim, soft nuts with an oily texture, these come from the Mediterranean stone pine tree. Pine nuts, also known as pine kernels, are used in pasta sauces, stuffings and salads and are usually browned before using. They turn rancid quickly, so store them in a refrigerator.

polenta Ground maize (corn) kernels mixed with water, made into a flat, golden loaf, sliced and grilled. Polenta needs to be flavoured as it is bland, although it is rich in vitamins. It can also be served in a softer form, like mashed potatoes.

pumpkin seed oil Pressed from roasted pumpkin seeds, this thick, brown oil, tinged with green, has a wonderfully powerful, toasted flavour.

puy lentils Small, round lentils, greenish brown in colour and far superior to any other lentil for texture and flavour. They come from the area around Le Puy in France.

risotto rice Arborio is the classic risotto rice from Piedmont. It absorbs a lot of cooking liquid without becoming too soft. The grain is plump and irregular, translucent at the edges with a hard, white core. It produces a creamy risotto with a slight bite. Carnaroli is very similar.

saffron The dried stigmas of a species of crocus, with a pungent aroma, bitter flavour and a beautiful golden colour. Buy it in Spain or at duty-free shops where it is cheaper and comes in larger containers.

sea salt I think Maldon sea salt from Essex is by far the best; there are no additives and the large, flaky crystals are fantastic on a salad or used at the table.

squashes These are members of the marrow and pumpkin family; the best is butternut squash for its sweet flavour and dense texture.

sun-dried tomatoes Intensely flavoured dried tomatoes that add zip to a dish. Those bottled in oil are more convenient to use than the dried variety, which need to be soaked before use.

truffle oil The infusion of truffle juices into an oil, usually extra virgin olive oil. White truffle oil is usually more expensive and stronger in flavour than black truffle oil. Use both sparingly as they have an intense flavour.

wild mushrooms

Chanterelles Wonderful aromatic mushrooms with a perfumed taste, chanterelles are shaped like open horns, torn around the edges. They vary in colour from brown to gold and dry well.

Morels Mushrooms with bulbous pitted caps and an intense aroma. Fresh morels need to be cleaned well. They are also found in dried and bottled forms.

Porcini Delicious mushrooms with a deep, rich flavour, porcini have a round, bun-like cap, a thick chubby stalk and fleshy texture. They are sold fresh and dried. Soak dried porcini in hot water for 15 minutes before use, then drain, filter and reserve the water to use as a rich stock.

Truffles The mysterious king of fungi, these are found below ground near oak trees and are sniffed out by pigs or dogs in autumn and winter. Usually the size of a walnut, truffles are rough on the outside, dense inside and firm to the touch. Both white and black truffles are found; their flavour is so intense that only a little is needed. Truffles are best served raw, finely shaved over salad or pasta.

soups

In Italy, soup is served as a *primo piatto*, first course, as an alternative to rice or pasta. Many of the soups are hearty, based on beans, vegetables and bread, and thus make complete meals in themselves.

spinach and broccoli soup

preparation time **10 mins**
cooking time **20 mins**
total time **30 mins** serves **4**

2 tablespoons olive oil
50 g/2 oz butter
1 onion, diced
1 garlic clove, crushed
2 potatoes, chopped
250 g/8 oz broccoli, chopped
300 g/10 oz spinach, chopped
900 ml/1½ pints chicken or vegetable stock
125 g/4 oz Gorgonzola cheese, crumbled
   into small pieces
juice of ½ lemon
½ teaspoon grated nutmeg
salt and pepper
75 g/3 oz toasted pine nuts, to garnish
warm crusty bread, to serve

one Heat the oil and butter in a saucepan, add the onion and garlic and sauté for 3 mins.
two Add the chopped potatoes, broccoli, spinach and stock, bring to the boil and simmer for 15 mins.
three This soup can be puréed or left with chunky pieces. Add the Gorgonzola to the soup with the lemon juice, nutmeg and salt and pepper to taste. Garnish with the toasted pine nuts and serve with warm crusty bread.

melon and parma ham soup

preparation time **10 mins**
total time **10 mins** serves **4**

1 ripe cantaloupe or charentais melon,
   weighing about 1.5 kg/3 lb
8 slices of Parma ham
salt and pepper
red basil leaves, torn, to garnish

one Cut the melon in half and remove the seeds. Scoop the flesh into a food processor or blender and whizz until smooth, then add salt and pepper to taste.
two Finely dice 4 of the ham slices and stir them into the soup. Cut the remaining 4 slices into thin ribbons.
three Garnish the soup with the ham ribbons and torn basil leaves.

Serve at room temperature or just slightly chilled. When food is too cold, you cannot taste its full flavour.

pesto and green vegetable soup

preparation time **10 mins**
cooking time **20 mins**
total time **30 mins** serves **4**

PESTO
3 garlic cloves, crushed
handful of basil leaves
2 tablespoons pine nuts
50 g/2 oz Parmesan cheese, freshly grated
3 tablespoons olive oil

SOUP
3 tablespoons olive oil
1 onion, diced
2 leeks, sliced
1 potato, chopped
425 g/14 oz can haricot beans, drained
    and rinsed
1.5 litres/2½ pints vegetable stock
2 courgettes, diced
125 g/4 oz small green beans, chopped
125 g/4 oz broccoli florets, chopped
250 g/8 oz canned artichoke hearts
1 tablespoon flat leaf parsley, chopped
salt and pepper

one To make the pesto, put the garlic, basil, pine nuts and Parmesan into a food processor or blender and purée thoroughly. Add the oil and blend again. Set aside.
two Heat the oil for the soup in a saucepan, add the onion and leeks and cook over a gentle heat for about 3 mins.
three Add the potato, haricot beans, stock and salt and pepper to taste, bring to the boil and simmer for 12 mins.
four Add the vegetables and simmer for 5 mins. Stir in the parsley and pesto and serve.

minestrone soup

preparation time **5 mins**
cooking time **25 mins**
total time **30 mins** serves **4**

2 tablespoons olive oil
1 onion, diced
1 garlic clove, crushed
2 celery sticks, chopped
1 leek, finely sliced
1 carrot, chopped
400 g/13 oz can chopped tomatoes
600 ml/1 pint chicken or vegetable stock
1 courgette, diced
½ small cabbage, shredded
1 bay leaf
75 g/3 oz canned haricot beans
75 g/3 oz spaghetti, broken into small pieces
1 tablespoon flat leaf parsley, chopped
salt and pepper

TO SERVE
50 g/2 oz Parmesan cheese, freshly grated
bruschetta (see page 20)

one Heat the oil in a saucepan, add the onion, garlic, celery, leek and carrot and sauté for 3 mins.
two Add the tomatoes, stock, courgette, cabbage, bay leaf and beans. Bring to the boil and simmer for 10 mins.
three Add the broken spaghetti and season with salt and pepper to taste. Stir well and cook for a further 8 mins. Keep stirring as the soup may stick to the bottom of the pan.
four Just before serving, add the chopped parsley and stir well. Serve with grated Parmesan and bruschetta.

butternut squash soup

preparation time **5 mins**
cooking time **25 mins**
total time **30 mins** serves **4**

1 butternut squash, weighing 875 g/1¾ lb
50 g/2 oz butter
2 tablespoons olive oil
2 onions, chopped
1 garlic clove, crushed
1 litre/1¾ pints chicken or vegetable stock
pinch of saffron threads
salt and pepper

TO SERVE
2 rosemary sprigs, chopped
75 g/3 oz Parmesan cheese, freshly grated

one To prepare the squash, cut it in half
and remove all the seeds, peel off the skin
and chop the flesh into small dice.
two Heat the butter and oil in a saucepan,
add the onions, garlic and squash and sauté
for 5 mins.
three Add the stock and saffron, bring to
the boil and simmer for 15 mins.
four Pour the soup into a food processor
or blender and work to a purée. Season
generously with salt and pepper.
five To serve, ladle into warmed bowls and
sprinkle each one with chopped rosemary
and a generous spoonful of grated Parmesan.

Like Minestrone, Tuscan bean soup can be reheated and, as it improves with keeping, it is really worth making the day before and storing in the refrigerator, allowing all the flavours to mingle.

mussel soup

preparation time **10 mins**
cooking time **10 mins**
total time **20 mins** serves **4**

2 tablespoons olive oil
2 onions, chopped
2 garlic cloves, crushed
1 red chilli, deseeded and chopped
150 g/5 oz piece of green bacon, chopped
1 kg/2 lb mussels, scrubbed and debearded
2 x 400 g/13 oz cans chopped tomatoes
½ bottle dry white wine
good pinch of saffron threads
handful of flat leaf parsley, roughly chopped
salt and pepper

one Warm the oil in a large saucepan.
Add the onions, garlic, chilli and bacon
and sauté for 5 mins.
two Check the mussels carefully. Discard
any that are open or do not close immediately
when tapped on a work surface.
three Add the mussels, tomatoes, wine,
saffron and salt and pepper to taste and mix
well. Place a tight-fitting lid on the pan and
simmer for 5 mins or until all the mussel
shells have opened. Discard any mussels
with shells that remain shut.
four Add the parsley, stir well and serve
at once.

tuscan bean soup

preparation time **5 mins**
cooking time **25 mins**
total time **30 mins** serves **4**

2 tablespoons olive oil
4 shallots, chopped
2 garlic cloves, crushed
150 g/5 oz piece of green bacon, diced
1 carrot, diced
2 celery sticks, diced
½ red pepper, cored, deseeded and diced
425 g/14 oz can borlotti beans, drained and
    rinsed
1 litre/1¾ pints chicken stock
1 bay leaf
1 teaspoon chopped oregano
1 teaspoon chopped marjoram
handful of flat leaf parsley, chopped
salt and pepper
extra virgin olive oil, to drizzle

one Heat the olive oil in a saucepan, add the
shallots, garlic, bacon, carrot, celery and red
pepper and cook, stirring occasionally, for
5 mins.
two Add the beans, stock, bay leaf, oregano
and marjoram, bring to the boil and simmer
for 15 mins. Skim off any scum that may
come from the beans.
three Taste and season well. Finally, just
before serving, add the chopped parsley.
four To serve, ladle into warmed bowls
and drizzle each one with a little extra virgin
olive oil.

bruschetta

preparation time **5 mins**
cooking time **5 mins**
total time **10 mins** serves **4**

8 slices of ciabatta bread
2 garlic cloves, peeled
small handful of flat leaf parsley, chopped
5 tablespoons olive oil
salt

one Toast the bread under a preheated grill until golden brown.
two Rub the garlic over one side of the bread; the bread acts as a grater and the garlic is evenly spread over the bread. Sprinkle the bruschetta with the parsley and salt to taste and drizzle with the oil. Serve immediately or keep warm until required, but do not keep warm for too long or the bruschetta will lose its crunchiness.

Bruschetta is delicious served with many different Italian dishes, especially soup and fish. It is a very useful accompaniment as the bread does not have to be fresh.

crostini

preparation time **10 mins**
cooking time **5 mins**
total time **15 mins** serves **4**

8 slices of ciabatta bread
2 garlic cloves, peeled
small handful of flat leaf parsley, chopped
5 tablespoons olive oil
1–2 red peppers, cored, deseeded, skinned
   and sliced into strips (see page 35)
75 g/3 oz black olives, pitted
125 g/4 oz goats' cheese, crumbled
salt and pepper

one Toast the bread under a preheated grill until golden brown.
two Rub the garlic over one side of the bread; the bread acts as a grater and the garlic is evenly spread over the bread. Sprinkle with the parsley and salt to taste and drizzle with the oil.
three Mix together the red peppers, olives and crumbled goats' cheese and season with pepper.
four Spread the mixture evenly over the toasted bruschetta and place under a preheated low grill for 2 mins to just melt the cheese. Serve at once.

variation Sliced tomatoes, sprinkled with chopped oregano and pepper, are also very good on bruschetta.

Crostini are an extension of bruschetta – the base is the
same but the crostini have many different toppings.
They are great with soup; if you want to serve a simple
supper, there is nothing better than a good home-made
soup, crostini with your favourite topping and a fresh
green salad.

pasta

Well over 200 different shapes of pasta are available in Italy and every region has its own particular specialities and ways of serving them. Pasta is one of the most versatile Italian foods and may be baked, stuffed and tossed in sauces or dressings.

pasta primavera

preparation time **15 mins**
cooking time **15 mins**
total time **30 mins** serves **4**

2 tablespoons olive oil
1 garlic clove, crushed
2 shallots, chopped
125 g/4 oz shelled peas
125 g/4 oz young broad beans, shelled
125 g/4 oz asparagus, trimmed
125 g/4 oz spinach, chopped
300 g/10 oz tagliatelle
150 ml/¼ pint whipping cream
75 g/3 oz Parmesan cheese, freshly grated
handful of mint leaves, chopped
salt and pepper

one Heat the oil in a saucepan, add the garlic and shallots and sauté for 3 mins. Add the peas, beans, asparagus and spinach to the shallot mixture. Stir well and cook for 2 mins.
two Meanwhile, bring a large saucepan of water to the boil. Cook the tagliatelle for 3 mins if fresh or 7 mins if dried, or according to packet instructions. Stir the pasta while it is cooking.
three Stir the cream into the vegetables, mix well and simmer for 3 mins.
four Drain the tagliatelle thoroughly, then add the pasta to the vegetable sauce and season well with salt and pepper. Add the Parmesan and mint and toss thoroughly with 2 spoons. Serve at once.

linguine with vegetables

preparation time **10 mins**
cooking time **10 mins**
total time **20 mins** serves **4**

1 red pepper, cored, deseeded and chopped
1 courgette, sliced
1 red onion, sliced
1 small aubergine, sliced into thin rounds
8 asparagus spears, trimmed
5 tablespoons olive oil
300 g/10 oz linguine
3 tablespoons frozen petits pois
125 g/4 oz Parmesan cheese, freshly grated
handful of basil leaves, roughly torn
salt and pepper

one Heat a griddle pan. Add the red pepper, skin side down, and griddle until the skin blisters and blackens. Griddle the courgette, onion and aubergine slices and the asparagus for 2 mins on each side. Alternatively, cook all the vegetables under a preheated hot grill.
two Peel the skin off the pepper and slice into ribbons. Place in a dish with the courgette, onion, aubergine and asparagus. Drizzle with oil. Keep warm in a low oven.
three Meanwhile, bring a large saucepan of water to the boil. Cook the linguine for 3–4 mins if fresh or 8 mins if dried, or according to packet instructions. Add the petits pois for the last minute of the cooking time.
four Drain the pasta and petits pois, then return to the saucepan. Add the vegetables, seasoning and Parmesan. Toss well, adding a little more oil if necessary. Add the basil and toss again, then serve immediately.

Cooking the vegetables for this dish on a heated
griddle pan or under a preheated hot grill intensifies
their individual flavours.

penne with tomato and chilli

preparation time **10 mins**
cooking time **20 mins**
total time **30 mins** serves **4**

3 tablespoons olive oil
1 onion, chopped
2 garlic cloves, crushed
2 pinches of crushed dried chillies
300 g/10 oz penne
10 plum tomatoes
1 teaspoon sugar
1 teaspoon vinegar
handful of flat leaf parsley, chopped
extra virgin olive oil (optional)
salt and pepper
75 g/3 oz Parmesan cheese, freshly grated,
   to serve

one Heat the olive oil in a saucepan, add the onion and garlic and sauté until soft; do not let them brown. Add the chillies.
two Meanwhile, bring a large saucepan of water to the boil. Cook the penne for 6 mins if fresh or 10 mins if dried, or according to packet instructions.
three Cut a cross at the stem end of each tomato. Place in a heatproof bowl and pour over boiling water to cover. Leave for 1–2 mins, then drain and peel off the skins. Cut the tomatoes into quarters, deseed, then cut lengthways into strips.
four Add the tomatoes to the onion mixture. Over a low heat, add the sugar, vinegar and salt and pepper to taste. Mix gently and simmer slowly until the pasta is cooked.
five Drain the pasta well. Stir the parsley into the tomato sauce. Add the sauce to the pasta. Mix well, adding a dash of extra virgin olive oil, if wished. Serve with Parmesan.

saffron bows

preparation time **5 mins**
cooking time **10 mins**
total time **15 mins** serves **4**

300 g/10 oz farfalle
25 g/1 oz butter
150 ml/¼ pint double cream
½ teaspoon saffron threads
salt and pepper
75 g/3 oz Parmesan cheese, freshly grated,
   to serve

one Bring a large saucepan of water to the boil and cook the farfalle for 3 mins if fresh or 6 mins if dried, or according to packet instructions.
two Heat the butter and cream in a small saucepan, add the saffron and gently bring to a simmer; the yellow of the saffron will explode into the cream and a fantastic subtle aroma will fill the kitchen.
three Drain the pasta well, place in a warmed serving bowl and pour over the saffron sauce. Season with salt and pepper and mix well.
four Serve the Parmesan at the table and sprinkle just a little over each portion.

fusilli with parmesan and pine nuts

preparation time **5 mins**
cooking time **15 mins**
total time **20 mins** serves **4**

300 g/10 oz fusilli
125 g/4 oz pine nuts
75 g/3 oz butter
2 tablespoons olive oil
75 g/3 oz Parmesan cheese, freshly grated
handful of basil leaves
salt and pepper

one Bring a large saucepan of water to the boil and cook the fusilli for 3–4 mins if fresh or 7 mins if dried, or according to packet instructions.
two Toast the pine nuts under a preheated medium grill or in a pan over a moderate heat. Watch them constantly and move them around to brown evenly.
three Melt the butter with the oil in a small saucepan. Drain the pasta well, then pour over the butter, season with salt and pepper and toss well.
four Turn into a warmed serving dish, sprinkle with the pine nuts, Parmesan and basil leaves and serve immediately.

pappardelle with olives and capers

preparation time **10 mins**
cooking time **15 mins**
total time **25 mins** serves **4**

125 g/4 oz black or green olives, pitted
2 pinches of crushed dried chillies
2 tablespoons capers, drained, rinsed and
  chopped
7 anchovy fillets, drained and chopped
4 large pieces sun-dried tomatoes, soaked in
  olive oil
300 g/10 oz pappardelle
large handful of flat leaf parsley, chopped
75 g/3 oz Parmesan cheese, freshly grated
salt and pepper

one Roughly chop the olives. Put them into a saucepan with the chillies, capers and anchovies. Chop the sun-dried tomatoes roughly and add them to the saucepan with 4 tablespoons of the olive oil.
two Gently heat the olive mixture for 4 mins until warm; do not let it fry.
three Meanwhile, bring a large saucepan of boiling water to the boil. Cook the pappardelle for 4 mins if fresh and 7 mins if dried, or according to packet instructions.
four Drain the pasta, then add the warmed olive mixture, parsley and Parmesan. Season with salt and pepper. Mix well with 2 spoons and serve. This dish can also be left to stand for a while and served at room temperature.

This dish is delicious and very good in the summer because of the fresh taste of the lemon and basil. If orzo is not available, another pasta shape can be substituted.

lemon and basil orzo

preparation time **10 mins**
cooking time **10 mins**
total time **20 mins** serves **4**

2 garlic cloves, crushed
large handful of basil leaves
5 tablespoons olive oil
rind and juice of 2 lemons
300 g/10 oz dried orzo
150 g/5 oz Parmesan cheese, freshly grated
salt and pepper

one Using a pestle and mortar or a food processor or blender, blend the garlic, basil, oil and lemon rind and juice together until smooth.
two Meanwhile, bring a large saucepan of water to the boil. Cook the orzo for 6–8 mins, or according to packet instructions.
three Add the Parmesan to the basil mixture, blend well and season with salt and pepper.
four Drain the pasta thoroughly. Add the pesto and mix well so that the sauce is distributed evenly throughout the pasta. Serve immediately.

penne with broad beans, asparagus and mint

preparation time **10 mins**
cooking time **18 mins**
total time **28 mins** serves **4**

500 g/1 lb asparagus, trimmed and cut into
   short lengths
4 tablespoons olive oil
300 g/10 oz penne
250 g/8 oz shelled broad beans or peas
75 ml/3 fl oz double cream
75 g/3 oz Parmesan cheese, freshly grated
4 tablespoons chopped mint
salt and pepper

one Place the asparagus on a baking sheet, brush generously with oil and season with salt and pepper. Place under a preheated grill and cook for 8 mins, turning as they brown.
two Meanwhile, bring a large saucepan of water to the boil and cook the penne for 6 mins if fresh or 10 mins if dried, or according to packet instructions.
three Cook the beans or peas in a separate saucepan of lightly salted boiling water for 2 mins.
four Drain the pasta. Pour the cream into the empty pasta pan over the heat, add the cooked beans or peas, grilled asparagus and Parmesan and season with salt and pepper. Return the cooked pasta to the pan, add the mint and toss well with 2 wooden spoons. Serve at once.

mushroom and mozzarella lasagne stacks

preparation time **10 mins**
cooking time **20 mins**
total time **30 mins** serves **4**

2 tablespoons olive oil
50 g/2 oz butter
2 onions, chopped
2 garlic cloves, crushed
500 g/1 lb mushrooms, sliced
4 tablespoons double cream
4 tablespoons dry white wine
1 teaspoon chopped thyme
8 sheets of fresh lasagne
2 red peppers, cored, deseeded, skinned and
   thickly sliced (see page 35)
125 g/4 oz baby spinach leaves, chopped
125 g/4 oz packet buffalo mozzarella cheese,
   sliced
50 g/2 oz Parmesan cheese shavings
salt and pepper

one Heat the oil and butter in a saucepan, add the onions and sauté for
3 mins. Add the garlic and cook for 1 min.
two Add the mushrooms, turn up the heat and cook for 5 mins.
three Add the cream, wine and thyme, season with salt and pepper and simmer for 4 mins.
four Bring a large saucepan of water to the boil, add the lasagne, a few sheets
at a time, checking that it does not stick together, and cook for 3 mins if fresh or
7 mins if dried. Remove and place 4 pieces in a well-oiled, large ovenproof dish.
five Place a generous spoonful of mushroom mixture on each piece of lasagne, add some red pepper slices and half of the spinach leaves and put another piece of lasagne on top. Then add the remaining spinach, a slice of mozzarella and top with a little more mushroom mixture. Finish with some Parmesan shavings. Place the lasagne portions under a preheated very hot grill and cook for 5 mins or until the mushroom mixture is bubbling and the Parmesan is golden.

This dish can be cooked in advance except for the final browning of the Parmesan. Reheat in a moderate oven for 20 mins, then grill until golden.

spaghetti vongole

preparation time **10 mins**
cooking time **20 mins**
total time **30 mins** serves **4**

1.5 kg/3 lb baby clams (vongole)
4 tablespoons olive oil
2 garlic cloves, crushed
125 ml/4 fl oz dry white wine
75 ml/3 fl oz double cream
500 g/1 lb spaghetti
large handful of flat leaf parsley, chopped
salt and pepper
freshly grated Parmesan cheese, to serve

one To wash the vongole, place them in a colander and submerge in a bowl of cold water. Shake vigorously, then lift out the colander and replace with fresh water. Repeat until the vongole are clean, then drain well. Check the vongole and discard any that are damaged or open.

two Heat the oil in a large saucepan over a low heat, add the garlic and vongole, cover and cook for 3 mins or until all the vongole have opened. Discard any that do not open.

three Lift the vongole out of the pan with a slotted spoon. Remove half of them from their shells and return any liquid to the pan. Set the vongole aside.

four Add the wine and cream to the pan and increase the heat to reduce the sauce.

five Meanwhile, bring a large saucepan of boiling water to the boil. Cook the spaghetti for 3–4 mins if fresh or 8 mins if dried, or according to packet instructions.

six Return the vongole to the sauce, stir well and simmer for 2 mins. Add the parsley and spaghetti, season and mix well, using 2 spoons to combine the spaghetti with the sauce. Serve with Parmesan.

spaghetti with lobster

preparation time **10 mins**
cooking time **10 mins**
total time **20 mins**   serves **4**

1 kg/2 lb cooked lobster, cut in half lengthways
4 tablespoons olive oil
2 shallots, chopped
8 plum tomatoes, skinned, deseeded and
   chopped
juice of 1 lemon
300 g/10 oz spaghetti
handful of chives, snipped
salt and pepper

one Remove all the meat from the lobster
and cut it into chunks.
two Heat the oil in a saucepan, add the
shallots and sauté for 3 mins. Add the
tomatoes and lemon juice, season with salt
and pepper and cook for a further 3 mins.
three Meanwhile, bring a large saucepan
of water to the boil. Cook the spaghetti for
3–4 mins if fresh or 8 mins if dried, or
according to packet instructions.
four Add the lobster to the tomato sauce
and stir, then reduce the heat and cook for
4 mins.
five Drain the pasta well. Add the sauce
to the pasta with the chives, toss with
2 wooden spoons and serve immediately.

tagliatelle with crab sauce

preparation time **5 mins**
cooking time **15 mins**
total time **20 mins**   serves **4**

2 tablespoons olive oil
2 shallots, chopped
200 g/7 oz crab meat
1–2 pinches of crushed dried chillies
grated rind and juice of 1 lemon
300 g/10 oz tagliatelle
4 tablespoons double cream
handful of chives, snipped
salt and pepper
75 g/3 oz Parmesan cheese, freshly grated,
   to serve

one Heat the oil in a saucepan, add the
shallots and sauté gently until soft, but do
not brown.
two Add the crab meat, chillies, lemon rind
and juice and salt and pepper to taste.
three Bring a large saucepan of water to the
boil and cook the tagliatelle for 3–4 mins if
fresh or 6 mins if dried, or according to
packet instructions.
four Add the cream to the crab mixture and
bring to the boil.
five Drain the tagliatelle well. Add the chives
to the crab mixture.
six Add the sauce to the tagliatelle, mix well
and serve with a bowl of grated Parmesan.

This dish makes an excellent
quick supper to serve to friends –
the addition of lobster makes it
really special.

pappardelle with prosciutto and porcini

preparation time **10 mins**
cooking time **15 mins**
total time **25 mins** serves **4**

2 tablespoons olive oil
1 garlic clove, crushed
250 g/8 oz porcini, sliced
250 g/8 oz prosciutto
300 g/10 oz pappardelle
150 ml/¼ pint whipping cream
handful of flat leaf parsley, chopped
75 g/3 oz Parmesan cheese, freshly grated
salt and pepper

one Heat the oil in a saucepan, add the garlic and porcini and sauté for 4 mins over a moderate heat.
two Cut the prosciutto into strips; try and keep them separate.
three Meanwhile, bring a large saucepan of water to the boil. Cook the pappardelle for 4 mins if fresh or 9 mins if dried, or according to packet instructions.
four Add the prosciutto, cream and parsley to the porcini and season with salt and pepper. Bring to the boil and simmer for 1 min.
five Drain the pasta, add to the sauce and toss well, using 2 spoons to mix evenly. Sprinkle with the Parmesan, toss well and serve at once.

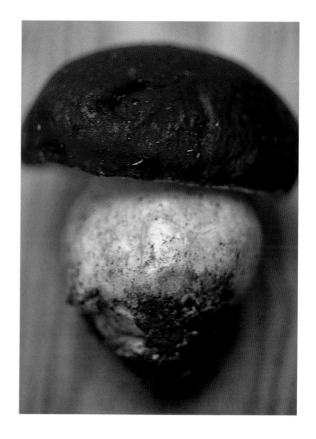

Fresh or dried porcini may be used for this recipe. If you use dried porcini, use 125 g/4 oz and soak them in hot water for 15 mins to rehydrate.

penne with chicken livers

preparation time **10 mins**
cooking time **10 mins**
total time **20 mins** serves **4**

1 yellow pepper, halved, cored and deseeded
300 g/10 oz penne
2 tablespoons olive oil
50 g/2 oz butter
1 red onion, sliced
250 g/8 oz chicken livers, trimmed
1 rosemary sprig, chopped
salt and pepper
75 g/3 oz Parmesan cheese, freshly grated,
    to serve

one Place the yellow pepper under a preheated hot grill for 5 mins, or until the skin is blistered and black. Allow to cool, then peel away the skin. Cut the flesh into long strips.

two Meanwhile, bring a large saucepan of water to the boil. Cook the penne for 4 mins if fresh or 8 mins if dried, or according to packet instructions.

three Heat the oil and butter in a large frying pan, add the onion and chicken livers and cook over a high heat until browned all over. Add the rosemary and season with salt and pepper. Do not overcook the chicken livers as this dries them out and makes them hard; they are best still pink in the middle.

four Drain the penne, add the chicken liver sauce and toss well. Serve immediately with a bowl of freshly grated Parmesan.

spaghetti carbonara

preparation time **10 mins**
cooking time **15 mins**
total time **25 mins** serves **4**

1 tablespoon olive oil
175 g/6 oz smoked bacon, rinded and
    cut into strips
1 garlic clove, crushed
300 g/10 oz spaghetti
4 tablespoons double cream
3 egg yolks
75 g/3 oz Parmesan cheese, freshly grated
salt and pepper

one Heat the oil in a saucepan, add the bacon and cook gently for 3 mins. Add the garlic and cook for 1 min.

two Bring a large saucepan of water to the boil and cook the spaghetti for 3–4 mins if fresh or 8 mins if dried, or according to packet instructions. Drain and return the pasta to the pan.

three Beat the cream and egg yolks together in a bowl, add to the bacon and mix well over a low heat.

four Add the sauce and Parmesan to the pasta, season with salt and pepper and toss well with 2 spoons. Serve immediately.

orecchiette with spicy tomato and pancetta sauce

preparation time **5 mins**
cooking time **20 mins**
total time **25 mins** serves **4**

2 tablespoons olive oil
1 onion, chopped
2 garlic cloves, crushed and chopped
125 g/4 oz pancetta, chopped
400 g/13 oz can chopped tomatoes
½–1 teaspoon crushed dried chillies
125 ml/4 fl oz red wine
300 g/10 oz orecchiette
handful of flat leaf parsley, chopped
handful of basil, chopped
salt and pepper
75 g/3 oz Parmesan cheese shavings,
   to garnish

one Heat the oil in a saucepan, add the onion, garlic and pancetta and sauté for 5 mins.
two Add the tomatoes, chillies and wine and simmer for 15 mins or until the sauce is rich and thick.
three Bring a large saucepan of water to the boil and cook the orecchiette for 3 mins if fresh or 6 mins if dried, or according to packet instructions. Drain well.
four Stir the parsley, basil and salt and pepper to taste into the sauce. Add to the pasta and toss well. Garnish with some of the Parmesan shavings and serve the remainder in a separate bowl at the table.

pasta bake with spinach and ham

preparation time **15 mins**
cooking time **15 mins**
total time **30 mins** serves **4**

2 tablespoons olive oil, plus extra
   for oiling
1 onion, chopped
1 garlic clove, crushed and chopped
750 g/1½ lb fresh spinach, washed and
   chopped
pinch of grated nutmeg
8 sheets of fresh lasagne
250 g/8 oz ham, chopped into large chunks
125 g/4 oz packet buffalo mozzarella cheese,
   thinly sliced
125 g/4 oz fontina cheese, grated
salt and pepper

one Heat the oil in a saucepan, add the onion and garlic and sauté for 3 mins.
two Add the spinach and mix well. Cook for 2 mins over a moderate heat, just so that the spinach starts to wilt. Add nutmeg, to taste and season with salt and pepper.
three Lightly oil a large, shallow baking dish, place a layer of lasagne at the bottom, followed by a layer of the spinach mixture, a layer of ham, then a layer of mozzarella. Repeat until all the ingredients are used up, finishing with a layer of lasagne and the grated fontina cheese.
four Place at the top of a preheated oven, 200°C (400°F), Gas Mark 6, and bake for 15 mins until golden brown and bubbling.

Because this dish uses fresh lasagne and is loosely
layered, it cooks through much more quickly than
traditional baked lasagne.

risotto

Traditionally, risotto is served in small portions in large, wide-rimmed soup plates and topped with grated Parmesan or pecorino cheese. Sometimes risottos are simple with just the addition of fresh herbs; other times they are more substantial, cooked with seafood, meat or vegetables. It is essential that the short-grained arborio or carnaroli rices are used for risottos.

risotto alla milanese

preparation time **5 mins**
cooking time **20 mins**
total time **25 mins** Serves **4**

1 litre/1¾ pints chicken stock
75 g/3 oz butter
1 tablespoon olive oil
2 onions, finely diced
425 g/14 oz arborio or carnaroli rice
½ teaspoon saffron threads
125 ml/4 fl oz dry vermouth or
   white wine
125 g/4 oz Parmesan cheese, freshly grated
salt and pepper

one Place the stock in a saucepan and
simmer gently.
two Melt 50 g/2 oz of the butter with the oil
in a large, heavy-based saucepan, add the
onions and sauté for 5 mins.
three Add the rice and stir well to coat each
grain with the butter and oil. Add enough
stock to just cover the rice and stir well.
Simmer gently, stirring frequently.
four When most of the liquid is absorbed,
add more stock and the saffron and stir well.
Continue adding the stock in stages and
stirring until it is absorbed.
five Finally, add the vermouth or wine,
Parmesan and the remaining butter in small
knobs and season with salt and pepper.
Stir well and serve immediately.

green risotto

preparation time **10 mins**
cooking time **20 mins**
total time **30 mins** serves **4**

1 litre/1¾ pints vegetable stock
125 g/4 oz butter
1 tablespoon olive oil
1 garlic clove, crushed and chopped
1 onion, finely diced
300 g/10 oz arborio or carnaroli rice
125 g/4 oz green beans, trimmed and cut into
   short lengths
125 g/4 oz shelled peas
125 g/4 oz shelled broad beans
125 g/4 oz asparagus, trimmed and cut into
   short lengths
125 g/4 oz baby spinach, chopped
75 ml/3 fl oz dry vermouth or white wine
2 tablespoons chopped parsley
125 g/4 oz Parmesan cheese, freshly grated
salt and pepper

one Place the stock in a saucepan and
simmer gently.
two Melt half of the butter with the oil in
a heavy-based saucepan, add the garlic and
onion and sauté gently for 5 mins.
three Add the rice and stir well to coat
each grain with the butter and oil. Add
enough stock to just cover the rice and stir
well. Simmer gently, stirring frequently.
four When most of the liquid is absorbed,
add more stock and stir well. Continue
adding the stock in stages and stirring
until it is absorbed. Add the vegetables
and vermouth or wine with the final amount
of stock, mix well and cook for 2 mins.
five Remove the pan from the heat,
season and add the remaining butter,
parsley and Parmesan. Mix well and serve
at once.

Fresh or dried mushrooms may be used for
this recipe. If you use dried mushrooms,
use 125 g/4 oz and soak them in hot
water for 15 mins to rehydrate. Use the
excess liquid as stock in the recipe, as it is
full of delicious flavours.

risotto with forest mushrooms and sage

preparation time **5 mins**
cooking time **20 mins**
total time **25 mins** serves **4**

1 litre/1¾ pints vegetable stock
125 g/4 oz butter
1 tablespoon olive oil
1 garlic clove, crushed and chopped
1 onion, finely diced
250 g/8 oz forest (wild) mushrooms, e.g.
   morels, porcini, chanterelles or common
   open mushrooms, halved or quartered
300 g/10 oz arborio or carnaroli rice
75 ml/3 fl oz dry white wine
1 tablespoon chopped sage
salt and pepper
125 g/4 oz Parmesan cheese, freshly grated,
   to serve
truffle oil, to drizzle (optional)

one Place the stock in a saucepan and
simmer gently.
two Melt half of the butter with the oil in a
heavy-based saucepan, add the garlic and
onion and sauté gently for 3 mins.
three Add the mushrooms and cook gently
for 2 mins. Add the rice and stir well to coat
each grain with the butter and oil. Add
enough stock to just cover the rice and stir
well. Simmer gently, stirring frequently.
four When most of the liquid is absorbed,
add more stock. Continue adding the stock
in stages and stirring until it is absorbed.
five Add the wine, remaining butter, sage
and salt and pepper and stir well. Serve with
Parmesan and drizzle with truffle oil, if liked.

red wine risotto

preparation time **5 mins**
cooking time **20 mins**
total time **25 mins** serves **4**

600 ml/1 pint chicken stock
450 ml/¾ pint Valpolicella or other red wine
125 g/4 oz butter
1 tablespoon olive oil
2 garlic cloves, crushed and chopped
2 red onions, chopped
300 g/10 oz arborio or carnaroli rice
250 g/8 oz field mushrooms, sliced
175 g/6 oz Parmesan cheese, freshly grated
salt and pepper

one Place the stock and wine in a large
saucepan and simmer gently.
two Melt half of the butter with the oil in a
heavy-based saucepan, add the garlic and
onions and sauté gently for 5 mins.
three Add the rice and stir well to coat each
grain with the butter and oil. Add enough
stock to just cover the rice and stir well.
Simmer gently, stirring frequently. When
most of the liquid is absorbed, add more
stock. Continue adding the stock in stages
and stirring until it is absorbed.
four When half the stock has been
incorporated, add the mushrooms and
season with salt and pepper. The rice should
be stained with the colour of the wine,
giving it a rich, dark red colour.
five When all the stock has been added, and
the rice is just cooked with a rich, creamy
sauce, add most of the Parmesan and the
remaining butter and mix well. Garnish with
a little grated Parmesan and serve with the
remainder of the bottle of red wine.

green herb risotto

preparation time **5 mins**
cooking time **20 mins**
total time **25 mins** serves **4**

1 litre/1¾ pints chicken or vegetable stock
125 g/4 oz butter
2 tablespoons olive oil
1 garlic clove, crushed and chopped
1 onion, finely chopped
300 g/10 oz arborio or carnaroli rice
handful of parsley, chopped
handful of basil, chopped
handful of oregano, chopped
handful of thyme, chopped
125 g/4 oz Toma cheese, grated
salt and pepper
herb sprigs, to garnish

one Place the stock in a saucepan and simmer gently.
two Melt half of the butter with the oil in a heavy-based saucepan, add the garlic and onion and sauté gently for 3 mins.
three Add the rice and stir well to coat each grain with the butter and oil. Add enough stock to just cover the rice and stir well. Simmer gently, stirring frequently. When most of the liquid is absorbed, add more stock. Continue adding the stock in stages and stirring until it is absorbed.
four When all the stock has been added, and the rice is just cooked with a rich, creamy sauce, add the herbs, the remaining butter and the cheese. Season and stir well. Garnish with herb sprigs and serve at once.

Toma cheese is made in the Italian Alps. If you cannot find it, use fontina or Parmesan instead.

butternut squash risotto

preparation time **5 mins**
cooking time **25 mins**
total time **30 mins** serves **4**

1 butternut squash, weighing 1 kg/2 lb
3 tablespoons olive oil
1 litre/1¾ pints hot vegetable stock
125 g/4 oz butter
1 garlic clove, crushed
1 onion, finely diced
300 g/10 oz arborio or carnaroli rice
150 g/5 oz Parmesan cheese, freshly grated
salt and pepper
pumpkin seed oil, to serve

one Top and tail the squash, cut in half around the middle, then pare away the skin from the larger half. Cut in half lengthways, deseed and cut into 5 cm/2 inch dice. Repeat with the other half. Place on a large baking sheet, drizzle with 2 tablespoons of the olive oil and season with salt and pepper. Mix well and cook in the top of a preheated oven, 220°C (425°F), Gas Mark 7, for 15 mins.
two Melt half of the butter with the remaining olive oil in a heavy-based saucepan, add the garlic and onion and sauté gently for 5 mins.
three Add the rice and stir well to coat each grain with the butter and oil. Add enough of the hot stock to just cover the rice and stir well. Simmer gently, stirring frequently. When most of the liquid is absorbed, add more hot stock. Continue adding the stock in stages and stirring until it is absorbed.
four Add the squash with the Parmesan, remaining butter and salt and pepper and stir gently. Serve drizzled with pumpkin seed oil.

seafood risotto

preparation time **10 mins**
cooking time **20 mins**
total time **30 mins** serves **4**

1 litre/1¾ pints fish stock
good pinch of saffron threads
125 g/4 oz butter
1 tablespoon olive oil
3 shallots, chopped
1 garlic clove, crushed and chopped
300 g/10 oz arborio or carnaroli rice
125 g/4 oz scallops, shelled and prepared
125 g/4 oz squid, cleaned and cut into rings
125 g/4 oz peeled prawns
2 tablespoons chopped flat leaf parsley
75 ml/3 fl oz white wine or dry vermouth
125 g/4 oz Parmesan cheese, freshly grated
salt and pepper

one Place the stock and saffron in a saucepan and simmer gently.
two Melt half of the butter with the oil in a heavy-based saucepan, add the shallots and garlic and sauté gently for 5 mins.
three Add the rice and stir well to coat each grain with the butter and oil. Add enough stock to just cover the rice and stir well. Simmer gently, stirring frequently. When almost all the liquid is absorbed, add more stock. Continue adding the stock in stages and stirring until it is absorbed.
four When half the stock has been incorporated, add the seafood. Increase the heat a little and add the remaining stock by the ladle, stirring carefully.
five When all the stock is absorbed, add the parsley, remaining butter, wine or vermouth, half of the Parmesan and salt and pepper. Serve with the remaining Parmesan.

spinach and lemon risotto

preparation time **5 mins**
cooking time **20 mins**
total time **25 mins** serves **4**

1 litre/1¾ pints vegetable stock
125 g/4 oz butter
1 tablespoon olive oil
2 shallots, finely chopped
300 g/10 oz arborio or carnaroli rice
500 g/1 lb spinach, chopped
grated rind and juice of 1 lemon
125 g/4 oz Parmesan cheese, freshly grated
salt and pepper
grated lemon rind, to garnish (optional)

one Place the stock in a saucepan and simmer gently.
two Melt half of the butter with the oil in a heavy-based saucepan, add the shallots and sauté gently for 3 mins.
three Add the rice and stir well to coat each grain with the butter and oil. Add enough stock to just cover the rice and stir well. Simmer gently, stirring frequently. When almost all the liquid is absorbed, add more stock. Continue adding the stock in stages and stirring until it is absorbed.
four Before you add the last of the stock, stir in the spinach, lemon rind and juice and salt and pepper to taste. Increase the heat, stir well and add the remaining stock and butter. Allow to cook for a few mins, then add half of the Parmesan and mix in well. Serve garnished with the remaining Parmesan and grated lemon rind, if liked.

The secret of a good risotto is to cook it
very slowly over a low heat until all the
liquid has been absorbed and the rice is
plump and tender.

pizza and polenta

Naples is reputed to be the original home of the pizza, but pizzas are now found all over Italy. Polenta is a yellow maize flour from northern Italy which can be baked, grilled, used as an accompaniment or is delicious with the addition of cheese.

It is very important to cook the pizza bases in a very hot oven, so do make sure to turn the oven on well in advance.

quick pizza base

preparation time **10 mins**
cooking time **see recipes** makes **4**

250 g/8 oz self-raising flour
1 teaspoon salt
150 ml/¼ pint warm water

one Place the flour and salt in a large bowl and mix well. Slowly add the water and mix to form a soft dough. When it has bound together, mix the dough with your hands into a ball. Turn the dough out on a lightly floured surface and knead until it is smooth and soft.

two Divide the dough into 4 and, with your hands and a rolling pin, flatten it as thinly as possible. The pizza rounds do not have to be exact circles as that is one of the charms of making your own pizzas! Make the pizzas just a bit smaller than your serving plates and as thin as you can.

classic tomato pizza

preparation time **8–10 mins**,
plus preparing the pizza base
cooking time **10 mins**
total time **30 mins** serves **4**

1 recipe Quick Pizza Base (see left)
3 tablespoons olive oil
2 red onions, sliced finely
2 garlic cloves, crushed
2 x 400 g/13 oz cans chopped tomatoes
1 teaspoon red wine vinegar
sugar, to taste
8 anchovy fillets, cut into thin lengths
2 tablespoons pitted black olives
1 tablespoon capers
250 g/8 oz mozzarella cheese, sliced
salt and pepper

one Roll out the dough to 4 circles or a large square.

two Heat the oil in a large saucepan, add the onions and garlic and sauté for 3 mins. Add the tomatoes, vinegar and sugar and season with salt and pepper. Increase the heat and simmer the mixture until it has reduced by half to make a thick and rich tomato sauce.

three Place the pizza bases on warmed baking sheets, spoon over the sauce and spread to the edge of the bases with the back of the spoon.

four Arrange the anchovies on the pizzas, sprinkle with the olives and capers and finally add the mozzarella. Put the pizzas into a preheated oven, 230°C (450°F), Gas Mark 8, and cook for 10 mins until golden and sizzling.

fresh wild mushroom pizza

preparation time **8–10 mins**,
plus preparing the pizza base
cooking time **10–15 mins**
total time **30 mins** serves **4**

1 recipe Quick Pizza Base (see page 50)
olive oil, for brushing
2 onions, finely sliced
2 garlic cloves, crushed
250 g/8 oz wild mushrooms, sliced
drizzle of truffle oil
salt and pepper
handful of flat leaf parsley, chopped,
    to garnish

one Put the pizza bases on to warmed
baking sheets and brush them lightly with
olive oil.
two Mix together the onions, garlic and
mushrooms and season with salt and
pepper. Spread the mixture over the pizzas
and drizzle with a scant amount of truffle
oil. Put the pizzas into a preheated oven,
230°C (450°F), Gas Mark 8, and bake for
10–15 mins.
three Sprinkle the pizzas with parsley and
serve at once.

artichoke and goats' cheese pizza

preparation time **8–10 mins**,
plus preparing the pizza base
cooking time **10–15 mins**
total time **30 mins** serves **4**

1 recipe Quick Pizza Base (see page 50)
2 onions, finely sliced
1 kg/2 lb artichokes in oil
2 tablespoons pitted black olives
175 g/6 oz mild goats' cheese, cut into thin
    slices or crumbled
handful of oregano, chopped
salt and pepper

one Put the pizza bases on to warmed
baking sheets.
two Mix together the onions and artichokes
and season well with salt and pepper.
three Divide the mixture between the bases
and spread over evenly. Sprinkle with the
olives and top with the goats' cheese,
oregano and salt and pepper. Put the pizzas
into a preheated oven, 230°C (450°F), Gas
Mark 8, and bake for 10–15 mins.

The addition of 50 g/2 oz of wild mushrooms, such
as chanterelles, to this pizza makes it really special.

anchovy and red pepper pizza

preparation time **8 mins**,
plus preparing the pizza base
cooking time **10 mins**
total time **18 mins** serves **4**

4 tablespoons olive oil

2 red onions, sliced

4 red peppers, cored, deseeded and cut into
  strips

2 garlic cloves, crushed

1 recipe Quick Pizza Base (see page 50)

50 g/2 oz can anchovies, drained

handful of marjoram, chopped

1 tablespoon black olives, pitted and chopped

250 g/8 oz buffalo mozzarella, sliced

salt and pepper

one Heat the oil in a saucepan, add the
onions and red peppers and cook for 5 mins
or until soft. Add the garlic and mix well.
two Put the pizza bases on to warmed
baking sheets, then spoon and spread the
cooked peppers over them. Arrange the
anchovies on top, sprinkle with salt and
pepper to taste, chopped marjoram and
olives and add the slices of mozzarella.
three Put the pizzas into a preheated oven,
230°C (450°F), Gas Mark 8, and bake for
about 10 mins.

fresh vegetable pizza

preparation time **20 mins**,
plus preparing the pizza base
cooking time **10 mins**
total time **30 mins** serves **4**

1 recipe Quick Pizza Base (see page 50)

5 tablespoons olive oil

2 garlic cloves, crushed

1 red onion, finely sliced

2 courgettes, thinly sliced lengthways

1 red pepper, cored, deseeded and cut into
  thin strips

1 yellow pepper, cored, deseeded and cut into
  thin strips

4 plum tomatoes, skinned, cored and cut into
  small wedges

500 g/1 lb asparagus, trimmed

4 thyme sprigs, separated into leaves

handful of basil leaves, roughly torn

salt and pepper

75 g/3 oz fresh Parmesan shavings (optional),
  to serve

one Put the pizza bases on to warmed
baking sheets, brush with a little oil, then
arrange the vegetables on the bases,
sprinkling them with the thyme leaves and
roughly torn basil.
two Season the pizzas generously with salt
and pepper, drizzle with the remaining oil
and bake at the top of a preheated oven,
230°C (450°F), Gas Mark 8, for 10 mins. The
vegetables should be slightly charred around
the edges as this adds to the flavour. Serve
with fresh Parmesan shavings, if liked.

spinach, parma ham and egg pizza

preparation time **15 mins**,
plus preparing the pizza base
cooking time **13–15 mins**
total time **30 mins** serves **4**

1 recipe Quick Pizza Base (see page 50)
olive oil, for brushing and drizzling
2 onions, finely sliced
2 garlic cloves, peeled and sliced
4 tomatoes, skinned and sliced
250 g/8 oz spinach, cooked and chopped
8 slices of Parma ham, cut into strips
1 tablespoon black olives, pitted and chopped
4 eggs
salt and pepper

one Put the pizza bases on to warmed
baking sheets. Brush them lightly with oil
and season with salt and pepper.
two Mix together the onions, garlic,
tomatoes, spinach, Parma ham and olives
and spread over the bases, making a nest in
the middle of each one for the egg.
three Drizzle the pizzas with the oil and
season with salt and pepper. Put into a
preheated oven, 230°C (450°F), Gas Mark 8,
and cook for 10 mins, then remove
from the oven and crack the eggs into the
nests. Return the pizzas to the oven for 3–5
mins, then serve immediately. If you like
your egg hard, put it on to the vegetable
topping when it first goes in the oven.

creamed polenta with dolcelatte and mascarpone

preparation time **5 mins**
cooking time **about 15 mins**
total time **20 mins** serves **4**

600 ml/1 pint water
150 g/5 oz quick cooking polenta flour
50 g/2 oz butter
2 tablespoons olive oil
175 g/6 oz dolcelatte and mascarpone torta
handful of oregano, chopped
salt and pepper

one Heat the water in a saucepan to a
gentle simmer, add the polenta and beat
well for 1–2 mins until it is a smooth paste.
two Turn the heat down and continue to
cook the polenta until it thickens, stirring
constantly so that it does not catch on the
bottom of the pan or form a skin on the top;
it needs to cook in this way for 6–8 mins.
three When it is thick and cooked, add salt
and pepper to taste, butter and oil and mix
well. The dolcelatte and mascarpone torta is
very creamy and wet; break it up into small
pieces and add to the polenta with the
oregano. Mix well.
four The polenta should now be the
consistency of soft mashed potatoes. Serve
on its own or with grilled chicken breasts.

Polenta has to be stirred continuously during cooking or it will become lumpy.

Use instant or quick cooking polenta for these recipes.

baked polenta with fontina

preparation time **10 mins**
cooking time **20 mins**
total time **30 mins** serves **4**

600 ml/1 pint water
150 g/5 oz quick cooking polenta flour
125 g/4 oz butter, plus extra for greasing
handful of marjoram, chopped
200 g/7 oz fontina cheese, grated
salt and pepper

SAUCE
3 tablespoons olive oil
2 garlic cloves, crushed
1 onion, chopped
400 g/13 oz can chopped tomatoes
1 thyme sprig
1 teaspoon vinegar
1 teaspoon sugar

one Heat the water in a saucepan to a gentle simmer, add the polenta and beat well for 1–2 mins until it is a smooth paste.
two Turn the heat down and continue to cook the polenta until it thickens, stirring constantly so that it does not catch on the bottom of the pan or form a skin on the top; it needs to cook in this way for 6–8 mins.
three When the polenta is thick and cooked, add the butter, chopped marjoram and salt and pepper to taste. Mix well. Place the polenta on a chopping board, roll out to 1.5 cm/¾ inch thick and allow to set for 5 mins. Alternatively, shape into a loaf shape and slice into 1.5 cm/¾ inch thick slices.
four To make the sauce, heat the oil in a saucepan, add the garlic and onion and sauté for 3 mins.
five Add the tomatoes, thyme, vinegar and sugar. Season with salt and pepper and simmer for 10 mins over a moderate to high heat until the tomatoes reduce to make a thick sauce.
six Butter a shallow ovenproof dish, cut the polenta into squares and line the bottom of the dish with half of the squares. Sprinkle over half of the grated fontina. Spoon over half of the sauce and top with the remaining polenta. Add the remaining sauce and the remaining grated fontina and bake in a preheated oven, 200°C (400°F), Gas Mark 6, for 10–15 mins until the cheese is golden and the sauce is bubbling.

grilled polenta with mushrooms and parma ham

preparation time **5 mins**
cooking time **25 mins**
total time **30 mins** serves **4**

600 ml/1 pint water
150 g/5 oz quick cooking polenta flour
125 g/4 oz butter
1 tablespoon olive oil
1 garlic clove, crushed
375 g/12 oz mushrooms, sliced
½ teaspoon chopped thyme
125 ml/4 fl oz dry white wine
8 thin slices of Parma ham
salt and pepper

one Heat the water in a saucepan to a gentle simmer, add the polenta and beat well for 1–2 mins until it is a smooth paste.
two Turn the heat down and continue to cook the polenta until it thickens, stirring constantly so that it does not catch on the bottom of the pan or form a skin on the top; it needs to cook in this way for 6–8 mins.
three When the polenta is thick and cooked, add half of the butter and season with salt and pepper. Mix well. Place the polenta on a chopping board, roll out to 1.5 cm/¾ inch thick and allow to set for 5 mins.
four Melt the remaining butter in a saucepan with the oil. Add the garlic, mushrooms and thyme. Sauté for 10 mins with the wine, to keep them moist. Season.
five Cut the polenta into wedges. Cook on a preheated griddle pan for 5 mins each side.
six Serve with the Parma ham draped over and mushrooms spooned over to one side.

rich polenta salad

preparation time **10 mins**
cooking time **20 mins**
total time **30 mins** serves **4**

600 ml/1 pint water
150 g/5 oz quick cooking polenta flour
25 g/1 oz butter
250 g/8 oz goats' cheese, rind removed
1 small radicchio lettuce, separated into leaves
125 g/4 oz rocket
3 tablespoons extra virgin olive oil
1 tablespoon balsamic vinegar
salt and pepper

one Heat the water in a saucepan to a gentle simmer, add the polenta and beat well for 1–2 mins until it is a smooth paste. Turn the heat down and continue to cook the polenta until it thickens, stirring constantly so that it does not catch on the bottom of the pan or form a skin on the top; it needs to cook in this way for 6–8 mins.
two When the polenta is thick and cooked, add the butter and season with salt and pepper. Mix well. Place the polenta on a chopping board, roll out to 1.5 cm/¾ inch thick and allow to set for 5 mins.
three Thinly slice or crumble the goats' cheese and arrange it on the polenta, then cut the polenta into bars or wedges. Place the polenta under a preheated grill and cook until the cheese has melted and starts to bubble.
four Put the radicchio leaves and the rocket into a bowl. Add the oil and vinegar and season with salt and pepper, then toss the leaves until coated. Arrange the salad leaves on individual plates and place the polenta bars on top.

The best goats' cheese to use for this
recipe is the rindless variety. Hard crusted
goats' cheese can be used, but it is not
as easy to spread.

salads

The majority of salads in this chapter can be main meals in their own right, but many make great accompaniments or starters, too.

When making this delicious but very simple salad dish, do try and cut all the ingredients into a similar size. This salad makes a great starter or a side dish to serve with a summer fish supper.

panzanella

preparation time **15 mins**
total time **15 mins** serves **4**

4 slices of ciabatta bread
4 ripe tomatoes
½ cucumber, peeled
1 red onion
handful of chopped flat leaf parsley
1 tablespoon chopped black olives
4 tablespoons extra virgin olive oil
1–2 tablespoons wine vinegar
juice of ½ lemon
salt and pepper

one Cut or tear the bread into small pieces and place them in a large bowl.
two Remove the green core from the tomatoes. Cut them up and add to the pieces of bread.
three Cut the cucumber into quarters lengthways and then into cubes. Add to the salad. Chop the onion and add to the bowl with the parsley and olives.
four Mix together the oil, vinegar and lemon juice and season with salt and pepper. Pour the dressing over the salad and mix well. Cover and leave to stand at room temperature for at least 1 hour before serving, to allow all the flavours to mingle.

caesar salad

preparation time **20 mins**
cooking time **5 mins**
total time **25 mins** serves **4**

1 garlic clove, crushed
4 anchovy fillets, chopped
juice of 1 lemon
2 teaspoons dry English mustard
1 egg yolk
200 ml/7 fl oz extra virgin olive oil
vegetable oil, for frying
3 slices of country bread, cubed
1 Cos lettuce, washed and torn into pieces
3 tablespoons freshly grated Parmesan cheese
pepper

one Place the garlic, anchovy fillets, lemon juice, mustard and egg yolk in a small mixing bowl and season with pepper. With a hand-held blender or small whisk, mix well until combined. Slowly drizzle in the olive oil, mixing all the time to form a thick, creamy sauce. If the sauce becomes too thick, add a little water.
two Heat the vegetable oil in a frying pan. Test with a small piece of bread to see if it is hot enough; if the bread sizzles, add the croûtons, turning them when they are golden. When they are cooked, transfer them to a plate lined with kitchen paper to absorb the excess oil.
three Put the lettuce into a large bowl, pour over the dressing and 2 tablespoons of the Parmesan and mix well.
four Serve the salad in a large bowl or on individual plates, sprinkled with the croûtons and the remaining Parmesan.

All the ingredients for this dish can be prepared in
advance, but never mix the salad until it is needed,
as the lettuce will go soggy.

This salad makes a tasty supper in its
own right as well as being an ideal
accompaniment to grilled meat or fish.

white bean and sun-dried tomato salad

preparation time **10 mins**
cooking time **5 mins**
total time **15 mins** serves **4**

2 tablespoons olive oil
1 onion, sliced
1 garlic clove, crushed and chopped
425 g/14 oz can white beans, drained
125 g/4 oz sun-dried tomatoes in oil, drained
   and roughly chopped
1 tablespoon chopped black olives
2 teaspoons chopped capers
2 teaspoons chopped thyme
1 tablespoon extra virgin olive oil
juice of ½ lemon
salt and pepper

one Heat the olive oil in a frying pan, add the onion and garlic and sauté over a high heat, stirring, to gain a little colour. When they are golden, remove from the pan.
two Put the beans into a mixing bowl and stir in the onion and garlic. Add the sun-dried tomatoes, olives, capers, thyme, extra virgin olive oil, lemon juice and salt and pepper to taste and mix well. Check the seasoning and serve.

tomato and green bean salad

preparation time **10 mins**
cooking time **2 mins**
total time **12 mins** serves **4**

250 g/8 oz mixed red and yellow baby
   tomatoes, plum if possible
250 g/8 oz thin green beans, topped and tailed
handful of mint, chopped
1 garlic clove, crushed and chopped
4 tablespoons extra virgin olive oil
1 tablespoon balsamic vinegar
salt and pepper

one Cut the baby tomatoes in half and place in a large bowl.
two Cook the green beans in boiling water for 2 mins, then drain well and place in the large bowl with the tomatoes.
three Add the chopped mint, garlic, oil and balsamic vinegar. Season with salt and pepper and mix well. Serve warm or cold.

caponata

preparation time **10 mins**
cooking time **20 mins**
total time **30 mins** serves **4**

6 tablespoons olive oil
2 aubergines, cubed
1 red onion, chopped
3 celery sticks, chopped
5 tomatoes, skinned and roughly chopped
3 tablespoons red wine vinegar
1 tablespoon sugar
1 tablespoon capers
50 g/2 oz black olives, pitted
handful of flat leaf parsley, chopped
salt and pepper

one Heat the oil in a saucepan, add the aubergines and fry until golden and soft. Remove from the pan and drain on kitchen paper.
two Add the onion and celery to the pan and sauté for 6 mins until soft but not brown.
three Add the tomatoes and cook for 3 mins, then add the vinegar, sugar, capers, olives, parsley and salt and pepper to taste. Simmer for 5 mins. Remove the pan from the heat, add the aubergines and mix well. Allow to cool, then serve.

aubergine, tomato and mozzarella mountains

preparation time **10 mins**
cooking time **10 mins**
total time **20 mins** serves **4**

1 aubergine, cut into 8 slices
4 beef tomatoes, skinned, then cut into
    8 slices
250 g/8 oz packet buffalo mozzarella,
    cut into 8 slices
2 tablespoons olive oil, plus extra for oiling
salt and pepper
mint sprigs, to garnish
Pesto (see page 16), to serve

one Arrange the aubergine slices on a preheated hot griddle pan or under a hot grill and cook until browned on both sides.
two Lightly oil a baking sheet.
three To prepare the stacks, place 4 of the aubergine slices on the baking sheet. Put a tomato slice and a mozzarella slice on each one, then make a second layer of aubergine, tomato and mozzarella, sprinkling each layer with salt and pepper as you go. Skewer with a cocktail stick through the centre to hold the stacks together.
four Place the stacks in a preheated oven, 190°C (375°F), Gas Mark 5, and cook for 10 mins.
five To serve, transfer the stacks on to individual serving plates and carefully remove the cocktail sticks. Drizzle with a little oil and top with a spoonful of Pesto (see page 16). Garnish with mint sprigs and serve warm or at room temperature.

Serve these 'mountains' with crusty Italian bread
to mop up the delicious pesto juices.

Serve this aubergine salad as a starter
or as an accompaniment.

piedmont peppers

preparation time **5 mins**, plus cooling
cooking time **25 mins**
total time **30 mins** serves **4**

4 red peppers
4–8 anchovy fillets
4 tomatoes, skinned and quartered
4 tablespoons olive oil, plus extra for oiling
salt and pepper

TO GARNISH
handful of green or red basil, roughly torn
125 g/4 oz Parmesan cheese

one Cut the red peppers in half lengthways.
Cut through the stalk first and then the
flesh. I always leave the stalk on as it looks
attractive. Remove the seeds and white ribs.
two Lightly oil a baking sheet and place the
peppers on it, skin side down.
three Cut the anchovies into halves or
quarters lengthways, depending how much
you like anchovies.
four Put 2 tomato quarters into each red
pepper, make an anchovy cross on top and
drizzle with oil. Sprinkle with salt and
pepper, place in a preheated oven, 200°C
(400°F), Gas Mark 6 and cook for 25 mins.
five Allow the peppers to cool, then serve
garnished with torn basil and Parmesan
shavings. Shave the Parmesan straight on
to the peppers, using a mandoline or a
vegetable peeler.

aubergine salad

preparation time **10 mins**, plus cooling
cooking time **15 mins**
total time **25 mins** serves **4**

4 tablespoons olive oil
1 onion, chopped
2 garlic cloves, crushed
2 aubergines, cubed
4 tomatoes, skinned and roughly chopped
4 anchovy fillets, chopped
2 tablespoons pitted black olives
75 g/3 oz pine nuts, toasted
2 tablespoons chopped capers
handful of flat leaf parsley, chopped
salt and pepper

ITALIAN SALAD DRESSING
1 tablespoon white wine vinegar
3 tablespoons olive oil
juice of ½ lemon
1 teaspoon Dijon mustard

one Heat the oil in a saucepan, add the
onion, garlic and aubergines and sauté for
15 mins.
two Meanwhile, make the salad dressing.
Place all the ingredients in a jar with a lid,
season with salt and pepper and shake well.
Set aside.
three Add the tomatoes, anchovies, olives,
pine nuts, capers and parsley to the
aubergine mixture and season with salt and
pepper. Pour in the salad dressing, mix well,
then allow the salad to cool before serving.

chicken and parmesan salad

preparation time **10 mins**
cooking time **15 mins**
total time **25 mins** serves **4**

2 boneless, skinless chicken breasts
1 garlic clove, crushed
150 ml/¼ pint olive oil
3 anchovy fillets, roughly chopped
juice of ½ lemon
1 teaspoon English mustard powder
1 egg yolk
1 Cos lettuce, torn into pieces
handful of basil, roughly torn
3 slices of ciabatta or white country bread, cubed and fried in oil
75 g/3 oz Parmesan cheese
pepper

one Place the chicken breasts on a preheated hot griddle pan or under a hot grill and cook on each side for 5 mins.
two Put the garlic, oil, anchovies, lemon juice, mustard and egg yolk into a food processor or blender, season with pepper and process until blended.
three Put the lettuce into a large bowl, pour in the dressing and toss.
four Arrange the lettuce on serving plates and sprinkle with torn basil leaves and the croûtons.
five Slice the chicken into long lengths and place on top of the lettuce. Shave the Parmesan on to the chicken with a mandoline or vegetable peeler and serve.

rocket, tuna and haricot bean salad

preparation time **15 mins**
total time **15 mins** serves **4**

4 tomatoes, skinned, cored and roughly chopped
125 g/4 oz rocket
425 g/14 oz can haricot beans, drained
200 g/7 oz can tuna in olive oil
1 red onion, chopped
125 g/4 oz artichoke hearts in olive oil
2 young celery sticks with leaves, chopped
1 tablespoon pitted black olives
juice of 1 lemon
1 tablespoon red wine vinegar
¼ teaspoon crushed dried chillies
handful of flat leaf parsley, roughly chopped
salt and pepper
warm crusty bread, to serve

one Put the tomatoes into a large salad bowl with the rocket.
two Stir in the beans and the tuna and its olive oil, roughly breaking up the tuna into large flakes. Stir in the chopped onion.
three Add the artichoke hearts and their olive oil, celery, olives, lemon juice, vinegar, chillies and parsley and season with salt and pepper.
four Mix all the ingredients together well and allow to stand for 30 mins for the flavours to mingle. Serve at room temperature with warm crusty bread.

figs with parma ham

preparation time **5 mins**, plus **5 mins** standing
total time **10 mins** serves **4**

4 figs
juice of ½ lemon
4 tablespoons extra virgin olive oil
handful of basil, roughly torn
12 slices of Parma ham, cut into paper-thin
    slices
salt and pepper

one Cut the figs into quarters and remove
the stems. Place them in a dish with the
lemon juice, oil and roughly torn basil leaves
and season with salt and pepper. Mix well
and allow to stand for 5 mins.
two Arrange the Parma ham on a serving
plate, then spoon the figs over the ham.
Sprinkle with salt and pepper and serve at
room temperature.

This recipe is very simple and relies
heavily on the quality of the
ingredients used, so it is best made
when figs are in season and then
only if they look ripe and delicious.
It is also important to buy your
Parma ham from a delicatessen
where the ham is carved to order.
If you like, the figs can be replaced
with a fragrant, ripe melon, peeled,
deseeded and cut into wedges.

vegetables

In Italy, vegetables appear at many different stages of the meal, as antipasti, in soups, as accompaniments and as main courses. Italy is blessed with an abundance of different vegetables including baby artichokes, asparagus, spinach and fennel.

If you have to wash the spinach, do make sure that it is dry before you start to cook. Place it in a salad spinner or tea towel, and spin it around to disperse any excess water.

quick spinach

preparation time **10 mins**
cooking time **10 mins**
total time **20 mins** serves **4**

1 tablespoon olive oil
1 red onion, sliced
1 garlic clove, crushed
75 g/3 oz pine nuts
4 tomatoes, skinned, cored and roughly
    chopped
1 kg/2 lb spinach, washed and trimmed
50 g/2 oz butter
pinch of nutmeg
salt and pepper

one Heat the oil in a large saucepan, add the onion and garlic and sauté for 5 mins.
two Put the pine nuts into a heavy-based frying pan and dry-fry until browned, stirring constantly as they turn very quickly.
three Add the tomatoes, spinach, butter and nutmeg to the onion and garlic and season with salt and pepper. Turn up the heat to high and mix well. Cook for 3 mins until the spinach has just started to wilt. Remove the pan from the heat, stir in the pine nuts and serve immediately.

fried courgettes with chillies

preparation time **5 mins**
cooking time **10 mins**
total time **15 mins** serves **4**

750 g/1½ lb courgettes, thickly sliced
75 g/3 oz plain flour
olive oil, for frying
50 g/2 oz butter
½ teaspoon crushed dried chillies
2 garlic cloves, crushed
rind and juice of 1 lemon
1 tablespoon green olives, pitted and chopped
salt and pepper

one Dust the courgette slices all over with the flour.
two Heat the oil in a frying pan and fry the courgettes, in batches, for 2 mins on each side until golden. Remove from the pan and keep warm.
three When all the courgettes are cooked, pour off the oil from the pan. Add the butter, chillies, garlic, lemon rind and juice and the olives and heat until the butter is foaming. Pour over the courgettes, season with salt and pepper and toss. Serve immediately.

courgette fritters

preparation time **10 mins**
cooking time **12 mins**
total time **22 mins** serves **4**

500 g/1 lb courgettes, trimmed and grated
1 garlic clove, crushed
50 g/2 oz Parmesan cheese, freshly grated
50 g/2 oz plain flour
1 egg, beaten
olive oil, for frying
salt and pepper
1 lemon, cut into 4 wedges, to serve

one Mix the grated courgettes, garlic, Parmesan, flour and beaten egg together in a large bowl and season with salt and pepper.
two Heat the oil in a frying pan. Place spoonfuls of the courgette mixture in the hot oil and fry for about 4–5 mins on each side or until golden and crispy.
three As the fritters are done, lift them out of the pan with a slotted spoon, pile in a warmed serving dish and keep warm. Keep cooking until all the courgette mixture is used up.
four Serve the fritters sprinkled with salt and accompanied by lemon wedges.

balsamic braised leeks and peppers

preparation time **5 mins**
cooking time **20 mins**
total time **25 mins** serves **4**

2 tablespoons olive oil
2 leeks, cut into 1 cm/½ inch pieces
1 orange pepper, cored, deseeded and cut into
    1 cm/½ inch chunks
1 red pepper, cored, deseeded and cut
    into 1 cm/½ inch chunks
3 tablespoons balsamic vinegar
handful of flat leaf parsley, chopped
salt and pepper

one Heat the oil in a saucepan, add the leeks and orange and red peppers and stir well. Cover the pan and cook very gently for 10 mins.
two Add the balsamic vinegar and cook for a further 10 mins without a lid. The vegetables should be brown from the vinegar and all the liquid should have evaporated.
three Season well, then stir in the parsley just before serving.

vegetable frittata

preparation time **5 mins**
cooking time **25 mins**
total time **30 mins** serves **4–6**

2 tablespoons olive oil
2 onions, finely sliced
2 garlic cloves, crushed
2 potatoes, boiled and sliced
2 red peppers, cored, deseeded and cut into
    strips
6 courgettes, sliced
1 thyme sprig, chopped
5 eggs, beaten
50 g/2 oz Parmesan cheese, freshly grated
salt and pepper

one Heat the oil in a frying pan with a heatproof handle. Add the onions, garlic, potatoes, red peppers and courgettes and sauté for 5 mins.
two Add the thyme, season with salt and pepper and mix well. Pour in the beaten eggs and cook over a moderate heat for 3 mins.
three Sprinkle with the grated Parmesan, put the pan into a preheated oven, 200°C (400°F), Gas Mark 6, and cook for 15 mins. The frittata should be set and golden on top.
four Remove the pan from the oven. Ease a palette knife all the way around the edge and under the frittata, slide it on to a large plate and serve at once.

The vegetables in this dish take on a wonderful
brown colour from the balsamic vinegar.

spinach and ricotta frittata

preparation time **5 mins**
cooking time **25 mins**
total time **30 mins** serves **4–6**

3 tablespoons olive oil
2 onions, finely sliced
1 garlic clove, crushed
5 eggs
500 g/1 lb spinach, washed and chopped
175 g/6 oz ricotta cheese
50 g/2 oz pine nuts
25 g/1 oz black olives, pitted and chopped
salt and pepper

one Heat 2 tablespoons of the oil in a frying pan with a heatproof handle, add the onions and garlic and sauté gently for 3 mins; do not brown.

two Beat the eggs in a large bowl and season well with salt and pepper. Add the chopped spinach and crumble in three-quarters of the ricotta. Add the pine nuts and olives and mix well. Add the onions and garlic and mix again.

three Heat the remaining oil in the frying pan, pour in the spinach mixture and cook for 5 mins.

four Sprinkle with the remaining ricotta and season with salt and pepper. Put the pan in a preheated oven, 200°C (400°F), Gas Mark 6, and cook for 15 mins. The frittata should be set and golden on top.

five To serve, ease a palette knife all the way around the edge and under the frittata, then slide it on to a large plate. This dish can be eaten hot or cold.

fennel baked with cream and parmesan

preparation time **5 mins**
cooking time **25 mins**
total time **30 mins** serves **4**

750 g/1½ lb fennel
small knob of butter
250 ml/8 fl oz double cream
75 g/3 oz freshly grated Parmesan cheese
salt and pepper

one Trim the outside leaves from the fennel, remove the hard central core and slice the fennel lengthways. Immerse the leaves in a pan of boiling water and cook for 5 mins. Drain well.

two Butter a shallow ovenproof dish, add the fennel and sprinkle with salt and pepper. Pour over the cream and sprinkle with the Parmesan.

three Place the dish at the top of a preheated oven, 200°C (400°F), Gas Mark 6, and cook for 20 mins. Allow the top of the fennel to go a deep golden brown.

baked young celery with parmesan

preparation time **5 mins**
cooking time **20 mins**
total time **25 mins** serves **4**

25 g/1 oz butter
2 small young heads of celery
handful of oregano, chopped
3 tablespoons olive oil
75 g/3 oz Parmesan cheese, freshly grated
salt and pepper

one Butter a large ovenproof dish. Cut the celery heads into quarters lengthways and place in the prepared dish. Add the oregano, drizzle with oil and season well with salt and pepper.
two Sprinkle the grated Parmesan over the celery and cook in a preheated oven, 200°C (400°F), Gas Mark 6, for 20 mins. The celery should become soft and the cheese golden and crunchy on top.

roast vegetables with olive oil and chillies

preparation time **5 mins**
cooking time **25 mins**
total time **30 mins** serves **4**

4 tablespoons olive oil
250 g/8 oz parsnips, cut into
   equal-sized chunks
250 g/8 oz leeks, cut into 1 cm/½ inch lengths
250 g/8 oz red peppers, cored, deseeded and
   cut into squares
250 g/8 oz aubergines, cut into chunks
½ teaspoon crushed dried chillies
handful of marjoram, chopped
salt and pepper

one Place the oil in a large roasting tin and put it into a preheated oven, 220°C (425°F), Gas Mark 7, for a few mins to warm.
two Add the parsnips to the tin, toss well in the oil, then return the tin to the top of the oven and cook the parsnips for 10 mins.
three Remove the tin from the oven and add the leeks, red peppers, aubergines and crushed chillies. Toss to coat in the olive oil, then return the tin to the oven to cook for a further 15 mins.
four Remove the tin from the oven and add the chopped marjoram and salt and pepper. Mix well and serve immediately.

stuffed aubergines

preparation time **5 mins**
cooking time **25 mins**
total time **30 mins** serves **4**

2 aubergines
4 tablespoons olive oil, plus extra for oiling
8 tomatoes, skinned and chopped
2 garlic cloves, crushed
4 anchovy fillets, chopped
1 tablespoon capers, chopped
handful of basil, chopped
handful of flat leaf parsley, chopped
75 g/3 oz pecorino cheese, grated
2 tablespoons pine nuts, toasted
50 g/2 oz white breadcrumbs
salt and pepper

one Cut the aubergines in half lengthways and scoop out the flesh without breaking the skin. Roughly chop the flesh.

two Heat the oil in a frying pan, add the aubergine shells and sauté them on each side for 3–4 mins. Place them in a lightly oiled baking dish. Add the aubergine flesh to the pan and sauté until golden brown.

three Mix the chopped tomatoes, garlic, anchovies, capers, basil, parsley, half of the pecorino cheese, the pine nuts, breadcrumbs and aubergine flesh together and season with salt and pepper. Spoon the mixture into the sautéed aubergine shells, piling it high. Sprinkle with the remaining cheese. Place in a preheated oven, 200°C (400°F), Gas Mark 6, and cook for 20 mins.

baked aubergine and gorgonzola

preparation time **5 mins**
cooking time **25 mins**
total time **30 mins** serves **4**

4 tablespoons olive oil
1 red onion, chopped
2 garlic cloves, crushed
400 g/13 oz can chopped tomatoes
1 red chilli, diced
handful of basil, roughly torn
2 aubergines, thickly sliced
125 g/4 oz Gorgonzola cheese
salt and pepper

one Heat 1 tablespoon of the oil in a saucepan and sauté the onion and garlic for 3 mins.

two Add the tomatoes and chilli and simmer for about 8–10 mins until the sauce has reduced. Add the basil and season well with salt and pepper.

three Heat the remaining oil in a large frying pan, add the aubergine slices and fry until golden on each side.

four Place a layer of aubergines in a shallow ovenproof dish and spoon over half of the sauce. Make another layer of aubergines, then add the rest of the sauce and finally crumble over the Gorgonzola. Bake in a preheated oven, 190°C (375°F), Gas Mark 5, for 15 mins.

sicilian aubergines

preparation time **5 mins**
cooking time **25 mins**
total time **30 mins** serves **4**

4 tablespoons olive oil
2 red onions, sliced
2 garlic cloves, crushed
2 celery sticks, chopped
1 aubergine, cut into small dice
1 yellow pepper, cored, deseeded and
   cut into thin strips
1 red pepper, cored, deseeded and cut
   into thin strips
150 ml/¼ pint passata
2 tablespoons red wine vinegar
6 anchovy fillets, cut into long strips
50 g/2 oz capers, roughly chopped
125 g/4 oz black olives, pitted
75 g/3 oz pine nuts
handful of flat leaf parsley, chopped
pepper

one Heat the oil in a heavy-based saucepan,
add the onions, garlic and celery and sauté
gently for 3 mins.
two Add the aubergine and yellow and red
peppers, turn up the heat and cook for a
further 5 mins, stirring constantly.
three Add the passata and vinegar and
bring to the boil, then reduce the heat so
that the mixture just simmers for 10 mins.
Add the anchovies, capers and olives and
simmer the mixture for a further 5 mins.
four Meanwhile, put the pine nuts into
a heavy-based pan and dry-fry until
browned, stirring constantly as they
turn very quickly.
five Finally, season the aubergine mixture
generously with pepper, add the pine nuts
and chopped parsley and mix well. Serve
hot or at room temperature.

broccoli with anchovies

preparation time **5 mins**
cooking time **10 mins**
total time **15 mins** serves **4**

75 g/3 oz pine nuts
1 kg/2 lb broccoli, cut into florets
50 g/2 oz butter
juice of 1 lemon
4 anchovy fillets, finely chopped
75 g/3 oz Parmesan cheese, freshly grated
salt and pepper

one Place the pine nuts in a heavy-based
frying pan and dry-fry until lightly browned,
stirring constantly as they burn very quickly.
Set aside.
two Steam the broccoli or plunge it into
boiling water for 2 mins, then drain well and
transfer to a bowl.
three Melt the butter in a small saucepan,
add the lemon juice and anchovies and heat
until the butter foams. Pour the melted
butter over the broccoli, sprinkle with salt
and pepper and toss. To serve, top the
broccoli with the Parmesan and pine nuts.

These potatoes are quite delicious and make an excellent
accompaniment to fish, or can be served on their own as
a starter. Alternatively, use very small potatoes and serve
them with drinks.

roast potatoes with rosemary and garlic

preparation time **5 mins**
cooking time **25 mins**
total time **30 mins** serves **4**

750 g/1½ lb medium potatoes, unpeeled
4 tablespoons olive oil
2 tablespoons chopped rosemary
4 garlic cloves, peeled and sliced
salt and pepper

one Cut the potatoes lengthways into quarters and make sure that they are thoroughly dry.
two Put half of the oil into a large roasting tin and place in a preheated oven, 230°C (450°F), Gas Mark 8, to warm through.
three Mix together the remaining oil and the rosemary and toss the potatoes to coat them completely.
four Add the potatoes to the roasting tin in the oven, shake carefully to give an even layer, then place the tin at the top of the oven and roast for 20 mins.
five Remove the tin from the oven and move the potatoes around so that they cook evenly. Scatter the garlic amongst the potatoes, return the tin to the oven and cook for a further 5 mins. Remove the potatoes from the oven, season with salt and pepper and serve immediately.

potatoes wrapped in parma ham

preparation time **5 mins**
cooking time **20 mins**
total time **25 mins** serves **4**

12 small new potatoes, cooked
12 very thin slices of Parma ham
2 tablespoons olive oil
sea salt

one Roll each potato in a slice of Parma ham, patting with your hands to mould the ham to the shape of the potato.
two Lightly oil a roasting tin, add the potatoes and cook in a preheated oven, 200°C (400°F), Gas Mark 6, for 20 mins. Keep an eye on the potatoes while they are cooking as they may need turning or moving around; often the ones on the edge get more colour than the ones in the middle.
three Serve sprinkled with sea salt.

Cavolo nero is an Italian cabbage with extremely long leaves, which is available in most of the larger supermarkets. It is almost the shape of a Cos lettuce, but the leaves are greeny purple in colour. Cavolo nero has a simple cabbage-like flavour but a slightly firmer texture. Like all cabbage, it is best not overcooked.

cavolo nero with pancetta

preparation time **5 mins**
cooking time **10 mins**
total time **15 mins** serves **4**

1 tablespoon olive oil
1 onion, sliced
1 garlic clove, crushed
1 red chilli, cored, deseeded and diced
125 g/4 oz pancetta, diced
1 head of cavolo nero
75 ml/3 fl oz chicken stock
75 g/3 oz Parmesan cheese, coarsely grated
salt and pepper

one Heat the oil in a large saucepan, add the onion, garlic, chilli and pancetta and sauté for 5 mins or until soft.

two To prepare the cavolo nero, trim any wilting leaves, then cut the heads in half lengthways. Remove and discard the hard central stem and roughly chop the leaves.

three Add the cavolo nero to the onion mixture and stir well. Pour in the stock and season with salt and pepper. Cook for 4 mins over a moderate heat, stirring constantly.

four Finally, add the grated Parmesan and serve at once.

braised broad beans and lentils

preparation time **5 mins**
cooking time **25 mins**
total time **30 mins** serves **4**

2 tablespoons olive oil
1 red onion, chopped
2 garlic cloves, crushed
125 g/4 oz pancetta or unsmoked bacon, diced
175 g/6 oz Puy lentils
1 kg/2 lb fresh shelled or frozen broad beans
handful of marjoram, chopped
8 fresh or canned artichoke hearts, prepared or
   drained
50 g/2 oz butter
handful of flat leaf parsley, chopped
salt and pepper

one Heat the oil in a heavy-based saucepan, add the onion, garlic and pancetta or bacon and sauté for 5 mins.

two Add the lentils, beans and marjoram, season with salt and pepper and cover with hot water. Mix well and simmer for 15 mins. The water may need to be topped up during cooking if the mixture is getting too thick and sticking on the bottom of the pan. Keep stirring, just to check that it does not stick.

three Add the artichoke hearts and cook for 5 mins. The mixture should be thick and rich. Finally, stir in the butter and parsley, taste for seasoning and serve immediately.

fish and shellfish

An abundance of fresh fish and shellfish is available in Italy. Chargrilling and simple cooking are the most popular methods of treating fresh fish.

grilled sea bass

preparation time **5 mins**
cooking time **7 mins**
total time **12 mins** serves **4**

extra virgin olive oil
2 x 1 kg/2 lb sea bass, filleted
salt and pepper

TO SERVE
2 lemons, halved
Braised Broad Beans and Lentils (see page 85)

one Lightly oil a baking sheet. Place the
4 sea bass fillets on the baking sheet and
drizzle with oil. Season generously with salt
and pepper and cook under a preheated very
hot grill for 7 mins.
two Serve with lemon halves and Braised
Broad Beans and Lentils (see page 85).

swordfish steaks in white wine and tomatoes

preparation time **10 mins**
cooking time **15 mins**
total time **25 mins** serves **4**

2 tablespoons olive oil
1 red onion, chopped
1 garlic clove, crushed
2 celery sticks, chopped
2 bay leaves
4 tomatoes, skinned and chopped
1 teaspoon sugar
300 ml/½ pint white wine
2 tablespoons chopped oregano
4 x 175g/6 oz swordfish steaks
salt and pepper

one Heat the oil in a pan, add the onion,
garlic and celery and sauté gently for
5 mins.
two Add the bay leaves, tomatoes, sugar,
wine and oregano and season with salt and
pepper. Mix well and bring to a gentle
simmer.
three Add the swordfish steaks and cook for
5 mins, then turn them over and cook on the
other side for a further 5 mins. This dish can
be served straight away, or in hot weather it
is very good at room temperature.

Choose a saucepan that the pieces
of fish will fit into as neatly as possible –
a frying pan may be best.

spicy fried sardines

preparation time **15 mins**
cooking time **10 mins**
total time **25 mins** serves **4**

oil, for deep-frying
125 g/4 oz plain flour
750 g/1½ lb large, fresh sardines, cleaned
4 tablespoons olive oil
5 shallots, sliced
125 ml/4 fl oz white wine vinegar
4 garlic cloves, crushed
large handful of mint leaves, finely chopped
rind and juice of 1 lemon
½ teaspoon crushed dried chillies
salt and pepper

one Heat the oil for deep-frying in a deep saucepan or deep-fat fryer. Season the flour with salt and pepper.

two Dip the sardines into the flour to coat evenly and fry in the hot oil for 2 mins or until golden. Remove and place on a tray lined with kitchen paper to absorb the excess oil. Keep warm.

three Heat 1 tablespoon of the olive oil in a saucepan, add the shallots and sauté for 5 mins, then add the vinegar and cook until nearly half of it has evaporated.

four Transfer the sardines to a warmed serving dish. Add the remaining olive oil, the garlic, mint, lemon rind and juice and chillies to the onion mixture and cook for 1 min. Spoon the sauce over the sardines and sprinkle with salt and pepper. This dish can be served hot or at room temperature.

tuna steaks with sun-dried tomatoes

preparation time **5 mins**
cooking time **15 mins**
total time **20 mins** serves **4**

2 tablespoons olive oil
1 red onion, finely chopped
2 garlic cloves, crushed
1 rosemary sprig, chopped
75 g/3 oz plain flour
4 x 175 g/6 oz tuna steaks
oil, for frying
125 g/4 oz sun-dried tomatoes, chopped
75 ml/3 fl oz red wine
1 tablespoon capers
75 g/3 oz black olives
handful of flat leaf parsley, chopped
salt and pepper
1 lemon, cut into 4 wedges, to serve

one Heat the olive oil in a saucepan, add the onion, garlic and rosemary and sauté gently for 5 mins.

two Season the flour with salt and pepper. Dip the tuna into the flour to coat evenly.

three Heat the oil for frying in a frying pan, add the tuna and cook for 4–5 mins or until golden. Turn over and cook on the other side for a further 4–5 mins. Transfer to a dish lined with kitchen paper and keep warm in the oven.

four Add the sun-dried tomatoes to the sautéed onions and stir well. Turn up the heat to high, add the wine, capers, olives and parsley and season with salt and pepper. Simmer for 2 mins. Serve the sauce with the tuna steaks and lemon wedges.

trout with parmesan and basil dressing

preparation time **10 mins**
cooking time **10 mins**
total time **20 mins** serves **4**

4 tablespoons olive oil
4 x 200 g/7 oz trout fillets
large handful of basil leaves, roughly chopped
1 garlic clove, crushed
125 g/4 oz Parmesan cheese, freshly grated
salt and pepper

one Lightly brush a baking sheet with oil
and place under a preheated very hot grill
to heat up.
two Put the trout fillets on to the hot tray,
sprinkle with salt and pepper and place
under the grill for 5 mins.
three Put the basil and garlic into a bowl.
Work in the oil using a hand-held blender.
four Remove the fish from the grill and
sprinkle with the grated Parmesan. Return
to the grill and cook for a further 3–5 mins or
until the Parmesan turns golden. Serve with
the basil sauce drizzled over the trout fillets.

grilled red mullet with salsa verde

preparation time **10 mins**
cooking time **15 mins**
total time **25 mins** serves **4**

4 x 375 g/12 oz red mullet, scaled and cleaned

SALSA VERDE
125 g/4 oz flat leaf parsley, chopped
125 g/4 oz basil, chopped
5 anchovy fillets, roughly chopped
2 tablespoons capers
2 garlic cloves, crushed
rind and juice of 1 lemon
150 ml/¼ pint olive oil
salt and pepper

one Make 3 slashes across the fish on each
side and season with salt and pepper. Place
under a preheated very hot grill and cook on
each side for 6–8 mins or until cooked.
two To make the salsa verde, put the
parsley, basil, anchovies, capers and garlic
into a food processor or blender and process
to a smooth paste. Add the lemon rind and
juice and oil, season with salt and pepper
and blend again.
three Remove the fish from the grill and
put a spoonful of the salsa verde into each
of the slashes on one side of the fish. Serve
the remaining salsa verde at the table in a
small serving dish.

Salsa verde, literally translated as green sauce, is traditionally
served with 'bollito mista', a north Italian dish of boiled meats
and poultry. It also tastes great on fresh bread.

fish casserole

preparation time **10 mins**
cooking time **15 mins**
total time **25 mins** serves **4**

3 tablespoons olive oil
2 red onions, finely diced
2 garlic cloves, crushed
½ teaspoon crushed dried chillies
200 g/7 oz squid, cleaned and cut into
   thin lengths
200 g/7 oz mussels, scrubbed and debearded
200 g/7 oz clams, cleaned (see page 32)
300 g/10 oz raw tiger prawns in their shells
150 ml/¼ pint fish stock
150 ml/¼ pint dry white wine
½ teaspoon saffron
8 tomatoes, skinned and deseeded
1 bay leaf
1 teaspoon sugar
500 g/1 lb red mullet fillets, cut into
   bite-sized pieces
handful of flat leaf parsley, chopped
salt and pepper

one Heat the oil in a saucepan large enough to hold all the ingredients. Add the onions and garlic and sauté gently for 5 mins. Add the chillies and mix well.
two Add the squid, mussels, clams and tiger prawns and stir well.
three Add the stock, wine, saffron, tomatoes, bay leaf and sugar and season with salt and pepper. Cover the pan and simmer gently for 5 mins. Discard any mussels or clams that do not open.
four Add the red mullet, sprinkle with the parsley and simmer for a further 5 mins, then serve at once. This is a very simple dish to make, but finger bowls are needed as it is very messy to eat. Serve with Bruschetta (see page 20) and a green salad.

halibut in paper parcels

preparation time **5 mins**
cooking time **25 mins**
total time **30 mins** serves **4**

1 fennel bulb
4 x 200 g/7 oz halibut fillets
2 shallots, finely chopped
8 pitted black olives
a few sage leaves, torn
4 lemon slices
salt and pepper

one Cut 4 sheets of greaseproof paper large enough to enclose the fish and vegetables.
two To prepare the fennel, trim the top and outer leaves, remove the hard central core and cut the bulb into slices through the root. Divide evenly between the sheets of greaseproof paper and put the fish on top. Sprinkle with the shallots, olives and sage, season with salt and pepper and finish with a slice of lemon. The greaseproof paper can be folded over and rolled at the edges to seal, but a much easier way is to fold the paper and staple it. Put the parcels on to a baking sheet and cook in a preheated oven, 200°C (400°F), Gas Mark 6, for 25 mins.
three Serve these parcels at the table so that everyone opens their own parcel and gets a waft of the delicious aroma that escapes when they are first opened.

roast monkfish with parma ham

preparation time **10 mins**
cooking time **15 mins**
total time **25 mins** serves **4**

4 x 175 g/6 oz monkfish fillets
4 rosemary sprigs
8 slices of Parma ham
2 tablespoons olive oil, plus extra for oiling
1 red onion, chopped
1 garlic clove, crushed
6 tomatoes, skinned, deseeded and roughly chopped
1 teaspoon capers, roughly chopped
handful of flat leaf parsley
salt and pepper

one Season the monkfish with salt and pepper, place the rosemary sprigs on the fish and wrap the slices of Parma ham around them. Put the fish in a lightly oiled baking dish and cook in a preheated oven, 220°C (425°F), Gas Mark 7, for 15 mins.
two Heat half of the oil in a saucepan, add the onion and garlic and sauté gently for 5 mins.
three Add the tomatoes and capers and mix well. Then add the remaining oil and parsley and season with salt and pepper.
four Serve the fish with some of the sauce spooned over one end.

roast cod with vegetables

preparation time **5 mins**
cooking time **25 mins**
total time **30 mins** serves **4**

750 g/1½ lb cod fillets, skinned
4 potatoes, unpeeled and quartered
6 tomatoes, halved
1 red onion, quartered
1 fennel bulb, cut into wedges
2 garlic cloves, crushed
75 g/3 oz black olives, pitted
25 g/1 oz green olives, pitted
25 g/1 oz capers
juice of 1 lemon
3 tablespoons olive oil, plus extra for oiling
salt and pepper
handful of flat leaf parsley, chopped,
     to garnish

one Put the cod, potatoes, tomatoes, onion and fennel into a large, lightly oiled dish. Try and arrange them in a single layer. Sprinkle with the garlic, olives, capers and lemon juice and season with salt and pepper.
two Drizzle with oil, place in the top of a preheated oven, 230°C (450°F), Gas Mark 8, and roast for 25 mins.
three Garnish with parsley and serve.

mussels with fresh tomato and pepper sauce

preparation time **5 mins**
cooking time **25 mins**
total time **30 mins** serves **4**

1 red pepper
2 tablespoons olive oil
2 red onions, chopped
2 garlic cloves, crushed
6 tomatoes, skinned and chopped
½ teaspoon crushed dried chillies
125 ml/4 fl oz dry white wine
1 kg/2 lb mussels, cleaned and debearded
2 tablespoons capers
large handful of flat leaf parsley, roughly
     chopped
salt and pepper

one To skin the red pepper, first cut off the bottom of the pepper. Put the pepper on a chopping board and slice off 4–5 flat pieces, leaving the seeds and core intact. Place the pepper pieces under a preheated hot grill and leave to blister and blacken, then peel off the skins and roughly chop the flesh.
two Heat the oil in a large, ovenproof casserole, add the onions and garlic and sauté gently for 5 mins; do not brown.
three Add the tomatoes, chillies and wine and simmer for 5 mins to reduce and thicken the sauce.
four Add the mussels and capers and season with salt and pepper. Mix well, cover with a lid and bake in a preheated oven, 200°C (400°F), Gas Mark 6, for 8 mins.
five Discard any mussels that have not opened, then stir in the parsley and serve.

tiger prawns with garlic and herbs

preparation time **5 mins**
cooking time **6 mins**
total time **11 mins** serves **4**

50 g/2 oz butter
2 tablespoons olive oil
750 g/1½ lb peeled raw tiger prawns
1 shallot, finely diced
2 garlic cloves, crushed
75 ml/3 fl oz dry white wine
125 g/4 oz flat leaf parsley, chopped
125 g/4 oz marjoram, chopped
salt and pepper

one Melt the butter with the oil in a frying pan, add the tiger prawns, shallot and garlic and sauté for 5 mins or until all the prawns have turned pink.
two Add the wine, parsley and marjoram and season with salt and pepper. Mix well and serve immediately.

This dish goes very well with egg pasta, or it can be served on its own with warm ciabatta bread to mop up all the juices.

pan-fried squid with chillies

preparation time **15 mins**
cooking time **6 mins**
total time **21 mins** serves **4**

1 kg/2 lb small squid, cleaned
4 tablespoons olive oil
3 garlic cloves, crushed
1 red chilli, finely chopped
juice of 1 lemon
handful of flat leaf parsley, chopped
salt and pepper

one Slit the squid down one side and lay them flat. Score the skin of each one with a fine criss-cross pattern.
two Mix half of the oil, garlic, chilli and lemon juice together in a non-metallic bowl and add the squid. Mix well to coat all over, cover and marinate for 15 mins.
three Remove the squid from the marinade, reserving the marinade. Heat a large frying pan or a wok with the remaining oil until it is just smoking. Add the squid, season with salt and pepper and stir well. Cook over a high heat for 2–3 mins. The squid will curl up, but just hold them flat for a few seconds to get a browned outside. Finally, add the strained marinade and the parsley to the pan, mix well and serve at once.

Chop the squid tentacles and use them in this dish as they
look very pretty. Their faint purple colour is subtly
complemented by the red chilli.

poultry, game and meat

High-quality meat and game are available throughout Italy, so often all that is needed is brief cooking and a sprinkling of olive oil, salt and black pepper. Older cuts are simmered in rich wine sauces to produce wonderfully tender dishes.

chicken livers with marsala and oregano

preparation time **5 mins**
cooking time **10 mins**
total time **15 mins** serves **4**

75 g/3 oz butter
50 g/2 oz pancetta or bacon, diced
1 shallot, diced
1 garlic clove, crushed
500 g/1 lb chicken livers, trimmed
175 ml/6 fl oz Marsala
1 tablespoon chopped oregano
salt and pepper
buttered tagliatelle, to serve

one Melt half of the butter in a large frying pan, add the pancetta or bacon, shallot and garlic and sauté gently for 5 mins; do not allow the shallot and garlic to colour. Remove from the pan.
two Melt the remaining butter, add the chicken livers and cook over a high heat for 3 mins until the livers are evenly brown on the outside. Chicken livers are best when cooked until browned on the outside but still pink in the middle.
three Return the shallot mixture to the pan and mix well. Add the Marsala and oregano and season with salt and pepper. Bring quickly to the boil. Serve immediately with buttered tagliatelle.

country chicken

preparation time **10 mins**
cooking time **20 mins**
total time **30 mins** serves **4**

50 g/2 oz butter
2 tablespoons olive oil
4 boneless chicken breasts
1 onion, chopped
½ small head of celery, chopped
1 garlic clove, crushed
½ teaspoon crushed dried chillies
300 ml/½ pint passata
1 bay leaf
thyme sprig
handful of oregano, roughly chopped
salt and pepper

one Melt the butter with the oil in a frying pan. When it is hot, add the chicken breasts and cook on each side for about 5 mins. Let them brown to add flavour to the sauce.
two Remove the chicken with a slotted spoon and set aside. Add the onion, celery, garlic and chillies to the pan and sauté for 5 mins.
three Add the passata, bay leaf and thyme. Season with salt and pepper and stir well. Return the chicken breasts to the sauce and simmer for 10 mins. Just before serving, add the oregano.

roman chicken

preparation time **5 mins**
cooking time **25 mins**
total time **30 mins** serves **4**

4 tablespoons olive oil
2 red onions, sliced
2 garlic cloves, sliced
2 red peppers, cored, deseeded and sliced
2 yellow peppers, cored, deseeded and sliced
½ teaspoon crushed dried chillies
8 boneless chicken thighs
100 ml/3½ fl oz white wine
large handful of basil, roughly torn
salt and pepper

one Heat the oil in a large frying pan, add the onions, garlic, red and yellow peppers and chillies and sauté for 5 mins.
two Add the chicken thighs, pushing them down to the bottom of the pan to seal on the outside. Cook for a further 5 mins.
three Add the wine and salt and pepper to taste, cover the pan and cook for about 15 mins over a low heat. Check occasionally that the chicken and sauce do not stick to the bottom of the pan and add a little more wine if necessary.
four Stir in the basil just before serving.

chicken with rosemary and garlic

preparation time **5 mins**, plus marinating
cooking time **15 mins**
total time **25 mins** serves **4**

2 tablespoons olive oil
2 tablespoons white wine vinegar
2 tablespoons chopped rosemary
3 garlic cloves, crushed
1 teaspoon paprika
pared rind of 1 lemon
4 boneless, skinless chicken breasts, cut into
    long thin strips
handful of flat leaf parsley, chopped
salt and pepper

one Mix the oil, vinegar, rosemary, garlic, paprika and lemon rind together in a bowl and season with salt and pepper. Add the chicken and mix well, then leave to marinate for 10 mins. Alternatively, this could be done the night before.
two Heat a large nonstick pan and add the chicken and the marinade. Mix well and cook over a moderate heat, stirring constantly, for 15 mins.
three To serve, stir in the chopped parsley.

black olive chicken rolls

preparation time **10 mins**
cooking time **20 mins**
total time **30 mins** serves **4**

3 garlic cloves, crushed
2 tablespoons capers
4 anchovy fillets, chopped
1 teaspoon thyme leaves
1 shallot, chopped
175 g/6 oz pitted black olives
1 tablespoon olive oil, plus extra for oiling
4 small boneless, skinless chicken breasts
salt and pepper
cooked pasta, tossed in olive oil, chopped flat
   leaf parsley and grated Parmesan cheese,
   to serve

one Put the garlic, capers, anchovies,
thyme, shallot, olives and oil into a food
processor or blender and whizz together.
two Place each chicken breast between
2 sheets of greaseproof paper and flatten to
about 2½ times its original size by pounding
with a rolling pin. Season the chicken
breasts with salt and pepper and spread
each one with a thin layer of the olive paste.
three Roll up the breasts and secure with
2 wooden cocktail sticks. Cut each chicken
roll in half and place in a lightly oiled
ovenproof dish.
four Cover with foil and cook in the top of a
preheated oven, 200°C (400°F), Gas Mark 6,
for 20 mins or until cooked. Serve with
pasta tossed in oil, parsley and Parmesan.

chicken stuffed with spinach and ricotta

preparation time **5 mins**
cooking time **25 mins**
total time **30 mins** serves **4**

4 boneless, skinless chicken breasts
125 g/4 oz ricotta cheese
125 g/4 oz cooked spinach, squeezed dry
¼ teaspoon grated nutmeg
8 slices of Parma ham
2 tablespoons olive oil
salt and pepper

one Make a long horizontal slit through the
thickness of each chicken breast without
cutting right through.
two Crumble the ricotta into a bowl. Chop
the spinach and add to the ricotta with the
nutmeg. Season with salt and pepper and
mix well.
three Divide the stuffing between the
4 chicken breasts and wrap each one in
2 pieces of Parma ham, winding it around
the chicken to totally cover the meat.
four Heat the oil in a shallow, ovenproof
pan, add the chicken breasts and sauté for
4 mins on each side or until the ham starts
to brown. Transfer the pan to a preheated
oven, 200°C (400°F), Gas Mark 6, and cook
for 15 mins. The ham should be browned
and slightly crunchy on the outside and the
chicken moist and soft.

rolled stuffed chicken breasts

preparation time **10 mins**
cooking time **20 mins**
total time **30 mins** serves **4**

4 boneless, skinless chicken breasts
4 slices of Parma ham
4 thin slices of buffalo mozzarella
4 asparagus tips, plus extra to serve
75 g/3 oz plain flour
1 tablespoon olive oil
50 g/2 oz butter
50 ml/2 fl oz dry white wine
75 ml/3 fl oz chicken stock
salt and pepper

one Place each chicken breast between 2 sheets of greaseproof paper and flatten to about 2½ times its original size by pounding with a rolling pin.

two Season the chicken with salt and pepper, place a slice of Parma ham, a slice of mozzarella and an asparagus tip on top and tightly roll up the chicken breasts. Tie with a piece of strong thread or spear with wooden cocktail sticks.

three Season the flour with salt and pepper. Dip the prepared chicken rolls into the flour to coat evenly.

four Heat the oil and half of the butter in a frying pan, add the chicken rolls and sauté over a low heat for 15 mins or until golden all over, turning frequently to brown the chicken evenly.

five Remove the chicken, place in a warmed serving dish and keep warm. Pour the wine and stock into the pan, bring to the boil and simmer for 3 mins.

six Remove the thread or cocktail sticks just before serving the chicken. Add the remaining butter to the pan, mix quickly with a small whisk to emulsify the sauce, then spoon over the chicken and serve with steamed asparagus.

duck breasts with balsamic vinegar

preparation time **5 mins**
cooking time **25 mins**
total time **30 mins**   serves **4**

1 tablespoon oil
4 boneless duck breasts
4 tablespoons balsamic vinegar
75 g/3 oz cranberries
50 g/2 oz brown sugar
salt and pepper

one Heat the oil in a frying pan, add the duck breasts, skin side down, and cook over a moderate heat for 5 mins. Reduce the heat and cook for another 10 mins. Drain the excess oil from the duck skin.

two Turn the duck breasts over and add the balsamic vinegar along with the cranberries and sugar. Season with salt and pepper and cook for a further 10 mins.

three Serve the cooked duck breasts with the sauce spooned over. The cranberries will have broken down and made a delicious sauce with the vinegar and juices from the duck. The duck breasts should remain pink and juicy in the middle.

grilled guinea fowl with fresh herb sauce

preparation time **10 mins**
cooking time **20 mins**
total time **30 mins**   serves **4**

4 boneless guinea fowl breasts
2 tablespoons olive oil
salt and pepper

HERB SAUCE
3 garlic cloves, crushed
4 anchovy fillets, chopped
large handful of flat leaf parsley
handful of rocket leaves
handful of sorrel leaves
handful of basil leaves
juice of ½ lemon
125 ml/4 fl oz extra virgin olive oil

one Put the guinea fowl breasts, skin side up, on a lightly oiled grill pan, brush with a little oil and season with salt and pepper. Place the pan under a preheated hot grill and cook the guinea fowl for about 10 mins on each side.

two Meanwhile, make the herb sauce. Put the garlic, anchovies, parsley, rocket, sorrel, basil and lemon juice into a food processor or blender and whizz for 1 min. With the motor running, slowly drizzle in the oil; the sauce should be thick and bright green with a strong, fresh aroma. Finally, season with salt and pepper and blend again.

three The guinea fowl is ready when the skin is crunchy and dark brown. Serve with a little herb sauce on each plate and the remainder at the table in a small dish.

braised breast of wood pigeon

preparation time **5 mins**
cooking time **20 mins**
total time **25 mins** serves **4**

75 g/3 oz plain flour
8 wood pigeon breasts, skinned
2 tablespoons olive oil
1 red onion, chopped
2 garlic cloves, crushed
3 celery sticks, chopped
250 ml/8 fl oz red wine
grated rind of 1 orange
1 thyme sprig
1 rosemary sprig
1 bay leaf
½ teaspoon ground cinnamon
2 teaspoons juniper berries, crushed
200 g/7 oz redcurrant jelly
handful of flat leaf parsley, chopped
salt and pepper

one Season the flour with salt and pepper. Dip the pigeon into the flour to coat evenly.
two Heat the oil in a wide saucepan, add the pigeon and cook for 2 mins on each side. Remove from the pan.
three Add the onion, garlic and celery and sauté for 5 mins. Increase the heat and pour in the wine, stirring well.
four Add the orange rind, thyme, rosemary, bay leaf, cinnamon, juniper berries, redcurrant jelly and salt and pepper to taste. Return the pigeon to the pan and baste well with the sauce. Simmer for 10 mins.
five Remove the pigeon from the pan and keep warm. Increase the heat and reduce the liquid to a rich glaze. Return the pigeon, add the parsley and serve.

quail with artichoke hearts

preparation time **5 mins**
cooking time **25 mins**
total time **30 mins** serves 4

75 g/3 oz plain flour
4 x 250 g/8 oz prepared quails
2 tablespoons olive oil
1 onion, chopped
2 celery sticks, chopped
2 garlic cloves, crushed
300 ml/½ pint white wine
handful of sage, chopped
400 g/13 oz jar artichoke hearts
salt and pepper
buttered pasta, to serve

one Sprinkle the flour on a plate and season with salt and pepper. Dip the quail into the flour to coat evenly.
two Heat the oil in a large saucepan, add the quail and brown all over. Remove from the pan and keep warm.
three Add the onion, celery and garlic and sauté for 3 mins, then pour in the wine, scraping any browned bits from the bottom of the pan.
four Return the quail to the pan with the sage and artichoke hearts and season well. Cover the pan and simmer for 20 mins, turning the quail from time to time. Serve with buttered pasta.

Serve the rabbit on a bed of pappardelle,
if liked. Pappardelle is the traditional
pasta to be served with game.

sweet and sour rabbit

preparation time **5 mins**
cooking time **25 mins**
total time **30 mins** serves **4**

75 g/3 oz plain flour
1 rabbit, cut into 8 pieces
2 tablespoons olive oil
1 onion, diced
1 garlic clove, crushed
300 ml/½ pint red wine
1 rosemary sprig
4 tablespoons balsamic vinegar
1 tablespoon brown sugar
2 tablespoons sultanas
2 tablespoons pine nuts, toasted
2 tablespoons black olives, pitted and roughly
   chopped
salt and pepper

one Season the flour with salt and pepper.
Dip the rabbit into the flour to coat evenly.
two Heat the oil in a large frying pan, add
the rabbit pieces, turning to brown them all
over, then remove with a slotted spoon and
set aside.
three Add the onion and garlic and sauté
gently for 5 mins; do not brown.
four Return the rabbit to the pan, pour in
the wine and add the rosemary, vinegar,
sugar and sultanas. Season with salt and
pepper. Simmer for 20 mins, turning the
rabbit frequently to coat it in the sauce and
to cook evenly.
five Just before serving, add the pine nuts
and olives and stir to mix well.

pan-cooked rabbit with sage

preparation time **5 mins**
cooking time **25 mins**
total time **30 mins** serves **4**

2 tablespoons olive oil
1 rabbit, cut into 8 pieces
handful of chopped sage
1 large rosemary sprig
150 ml/¼ pint dry white wine
1 tablespoon Dijon mustard
salt and pepper
handful of flat leaf parsley, roughly chopped,
   to serve

one Heat the oil in a large frying pan, add
the rabbit and brown all over.
two Season well with salt and pepper.
Add the sage, rosemary, wine and mustard,
mix thoroughly and coat the rabbit in the
wine sauce.
three Simmer the rabbit for 20 mins, turning
frequently so that it cooks evenly.
four To serve, sprinkle the rabbit generously
with the chopped parsley.

grilled fillet of venison

preparation time **10 mins**
cooking time **15 mins**
total time **25 mins**   serves **4**

4 x 175 g/6 oz venison fillet steaks
2 tablespoons olive oil, plus extra for sautéeing
1 shallot, finely chopped
2 garlic cloves, crushed
250 ml/8 fl oz red wine
4 cloves
1 piece of cinnamon stick
pared rind of 1 orange
10 juniper berries, crushed
3 tablespoons redcurrant jelly
salt and pepper
buttered pasta or Creamed Polenta with
    Dolcelatte and Mascarpone (see page 54),
    to serve

one Brush the venison steaks with the oil and season well with salt and pepper.
two Heat a little oil in a saucepan, add the shallot and garlic and sauté for 3 mins. Add the wine, cloves, cinnamon, orange rind, juniper berries and redcurrant jelly and simmer until it reduces to a rich sauce.
three While the sauce is cooking, place the venison fillets on a grill rack and cook under a preheated hot grill for 6 mins on each side.
four To serve, strain the sauce and spoon over the venison steaks. Serve with buttered pasta or Creamed Polenta with Dolcelatte and Mascarpone (see page 54).

roast pork fillet with rosemary and fennel

preparation time **5 mins**
cooking time **25 mins**
total time **30 mins**   serves **4**

1 large rosemary sprig
3 garlic cloves, peeled
750 g/1½ lb pork fillet, trimmed
4 tablespoons olive oil
2 fennel bulbs, trimmed and cut into wedges,
    central core removed
150 ml/¼ pint white wine
75 g/3 oz mascarpone cheese
salt and pepper
rosemary sprigs, to garnish

one Break the rosemary into short lengths and cut the garlic into slices. Pierce the pork with a sharp knife and insert the pieces of rosemary and garlic evenly all over the fillet.
two Heat half of the oil in a frying pan, add the pork and fry for 5 mins or until browned all over.
three Lightly oil a roasting tin, add the fennel and drizzle with the remaining oil. Place the pork on top, season generously and roast in a preheated oven, 230°C (450°F), Gas Mark 8, for 20 mins.
four Pour the wine into the frying pan and simmer until reduced by half. Stir in the mascarpone and salt and pepper to taste.
five To serve, cut the pork into slices and arrange on a warmed serving dish with fennel wedges. Pour the sauce into the roasting pan and place on the heat. Using a wooden spoon, stir all the tasty bits into the sauce, then spoon over the pork and fennel. Garnish with rosemary sprigs.

Thin green beans simply cooked in boiling water
for 2 mins complement this rich and tasty dish.

parmesan breaded lamb chops

preparation time **10 mins**
cooking time **10 mins**
total time **20 mins** serves **4**

75 g/3 oz plain flour
8 lamb chops, trimmed
50 g/2 oz Parmesan cheese, freshly grated
50 g/2 oz fresh breadcrumbs
2 eggs, beaten
2 tablespoons olive oil
salt and pepper
1 lemon, cut into 4 wedges, to serve

one Season the flour with salt and pepper. Dip the lamb chops into the flour to coat evenly. Mix together the Parmesan and breadcrumbs in a shallow dish and season with salt and pepper.

two Dip the cutlets first into the beaten egg and then into the Parmesan mixture to coat all over, pressing the crumbs on to the lamb.

three Heat the oil in a frying pan, add the lamb chops and cook on each side for 4 mins or until golden. Take care when turning them over; a palette knife is best, so as not to loosen any of the cheesy crust from the chops.

four Serve immediately with lemon wedges.

fillet steak wrapped in parma ham

preparation time **10 mins**
cooking time **8 mins**
total time **18 mins** serves **4**

handful of chopped marjoram
2 garlic cloves, crushed
4 x 175 g/6 oz fillet steaks
8 slices of Parma ham
125 g/4 oz buffalo mozzarella, cut into
   4 slices
salt and pepper

one Mix together the marjoram and garlic and season with salt and pepper. Coat the steaks with the herb mixture, then wrap them in the Parma ham. Make sure that all the steak is covered with the ham.

two Put the steaks on a greased grill rack and place under a preheated very hot grill, as close to the heat as possible without burning them. Cook for 3 mins on each side if you like your steak rare, 5–6 mins for medium and 8 mins for well done.

three Place the slices of mozzarella on the steaks, return to the grill and cook until the mozzarella is melting and just turning golden.

four Remove the steaks from the grill and leave to rest for 5 mins before serving. This allows the meat to relax.

breaded veal escalopes with parma ham and parmesan

preparation time **10 mins**
cooking time **10 mins**
total time **20 mins** serves **4**

4 x 175 g/6 oz veal escalopes
75 g/3 oz plain flour
2 eggs, beaten
175 g/6 oz fresh breadcrumbs
75 g/3 oz butter
50 g/2 oz Parma ham
50 g/2 oz Parmesan cheese, freshly grated
salt and pepper
handful of flat leaf parsley, to garnish
1 lemon, cut into 4 wedges, to serve

one Place the veal escalopes between 2 sheets of greaseproof paper and flatten them by pounding with a rolling pin.
two Season the flour with salt and pepper. Dip the escalopes first into the flour, then into the beaten egg and finally into the breadcrumbs to coat evenly.
three Melt the butter in a large frying pan. When it is foaming, add the escalopes and cook for 1–2 mins on each side until golden.
four Place the escalopes on a grill pan. Put a piece of Parma ham on each one and sprinkle with grated Parmesan. Place the escalopes under a preheated very hot grill and cook for 4–5 mins until the Parmesan is golden.
five Garnish the escalopes with chopped parsley and serve with lemon wedges.

veal escalopes with lemon and pine nuts

preparation time **10 mins**
cooking time **10 mins**
total time **20 mins** serves **4**

75 g/3 oz plain flour
4 x 175 g/6 oz veal escalopes
50 g/2 oz butter
1 tablespoon olive oil
75 g/3 oz pine nuts
rind and juice of 1 lemon
75 ml/3 fl oz chicken stock
handful of parsley, finely chopped
salt and pepper
Risotto alla Milanese (see page 40), to serve

one Season the flour with salt and pepper. Dip the veal escalopes into the flour to coat evenly.
two Heat the butter and oil in a frying pan. When it is foaming, add the escalopes and cook for 3 mins on each side or until golden.
three Sprinkle the pine nuts into the pan and stir until golden.
four Add the lemon rind and juice, stock and parsley and season with salt and pepper. Bring to the boil and mix well. Serve immediately with Risotto alla Milanese (see page 40).

It is important that all the ingredients for the
gremolata are finely chopped or grated as they
mix together better, making a more subtle blend.

veal chops
with gremolata

preparation time **5 mins**
cooking time **25 mins**
total time **30 mins** serves **4**

4 thin veal chops
75 g/3 oz seasoned flour
50 g/2 oz butter
1 tablespoon olive oil
2 onions, chopped
2 garlic cloves, crushed
2 celery sticks, chopped
1 carrot, chopped
2 bay leaves
6 tomatoes, skinned, deseeded and chopped
125 ml/4 fl oz chicken stock
125 ml/4 fl oz dry white wine
salt and pepper

GREMOLATA
2 tablespoons finely chopped parsley
1 tablespoon finely chopped sage
rind of 3 lemons, finely grated
3 large garlic cloves, crushed

one Coat both sides of the veal chops with seasoned flour. Melt the butter with the oil in a flameproof casserole, add the chops and brown well on each side. Remove from the casserole and keep warm.

two Add the onions, garlic, celery and carrot to the pan and sauté for 3 mins.

three Add the bay leaves, tomatoes, stock, wine and salt and pepper to taste, mix well and bring to the boil. Return the chops to the casserole and turn to coat them in the sauce. Cover and cook in a preheated oven, 200°C (400°F), Gas Mark 6, for 20 mins.

four While the chops are cooking, make the gremolata. Mix together all the ingredients in a bowl.

five To serve, transfer the chops to a warmed serving plate and keep them warm. Boil the sauce to reduce if necessary, then pour it over the chops and spoon some of the gremolata over each one.

desserts

This chapter includes some classic Italian desserts as well as some unusual new ideas including sweet and chocolate risottos.

This dish is best made the night before so that it can set completely.

tiramisu with raspberry surprise

preparation time **15 mins**, plus chilling
total time **15 mins** serves **4**

4 tablespoons very strong espresso coffee
2 tablespoons grappa or brandy
10 sponge fingers
125 g/4 oz raspberries
175 g/6 oz mascarpone cheese
2 eggs, separated
50 g/2 oz icing sugar
25 g/1 oz dark chocolate

one Combine the coffee and grappa or brandy in a bowl. Dip the sponge fingers into the liquid to coat evenly, then arrange them on a small shallow dish or a serving platter, pouring over any excess liquid. Sprinkle the raspberries evenly over the soaked sponge fingers.

two Whisk the mascarpone, egg yolks and icing sugar together in a bowl until smooth and well blended.

three In a separate bowl, whisk the egg whites until stiff and glossy, then fold the egg whites and the mascarpone mixture together until well blended.

four Spoon the mixture over the sponge fingers and smooth the surface. Finely grate the chocolate straight on to the mixture. Cover and chill until set.

zabaglione

preparation time **5 mins**
cooking time **10 mins**
total time **15 mins** serves **4**

4 egg yolks
75 g/3 oz caster sugar, plus extra for frosting the glasses
grated rind of ½ lemon
½ teaspoon ground cinnamon, plus extra to decorate
1 drop of vanilla extract
150 ml/¼ pint Marsala
125 g/4 oz fresh fruit (such as peaches, apricots and berries), sliced

one Place the egg yolks, caster sugar, lemon rind, cinnamon and vanilla extract in a heatproof bowl and beat with an electric whisk until thick, pale and creamy.

two Place the bowl over a saucepan of simmering water and continue whisking. Slowly add the Marsala and whisk until the mixture is warm, frothy and thick.

three To serve, dip the rims of 4 glasses in water, then in sugar to frost them. Divide the fruit between the glasses, then spoon in the zabaglione. Dust with a little extra cinnamon before serving.

This dessert is very good if made the night before to allow all the flavours to blend together.

italian trifle

preparation time **10 mins**
cooking time **10 mins**
total time **20 mins** serves **4**

8 sponge fingers
2 tablespoons blueberry jam
50 ml/2 fl oz Marsala or sherry
250 g/8 oz blueberries
300 ml/½ pint milk
1 tablespoon cornflour
2 egg yolks
2 tablespoons sugar
300 ml/½ pint whipping cream
50 g/2 oz chocolate, grated

one Spread the sponge fingers with the jam and arrange in a glass serving bowl. Sprinkle over the Marsala or sherry and add half of the blueberries.
two Mix a little milk with the cornflour to make a smooth paste. Stir the paste into the remainder of the milk. Pour into a saucepan and bring to the boil, stirring constantly as the milk will thicken. When it is boiling and smooth, remove it from the heat.
three Whisk the egg yolks and sugar together in a large bowl until they are light and creamy. Add the thickened milk to the beaten egg mixture, whisking constantly. Blend well and pour over the blueberries, then top with the remaining blueberries. Allow to cool.
four Softly whip the cream and spread over the trifle, then top with the grated chocolate.

blood orange granita

preparation time **10 mins**, plus freezing
total time **10 mins** serves **4**

1 kg/2 lb blood oranges
250 g/8 oz sugar

one Using a sharp knife, cut off the top and bottom of the oranges, then cut away the pith and peel. Working over a bowl to catch the juice, cut the segments out of the oranges and squeeze any excess juice from each one.
two Strain the juice into a saucepan, add the sugar and heat until it has dissolved.
three Place the orange flesh in a food processor or blender and whizz until smooth. Mix in the juice and pour into ice cube trays to freeze.
four When you serve the granita, first chill the serving dishes for a short while in the freezer. To serve, remove the granita ice cubes from the freezer, put them into the food processor or blender and whizz for 30 seconds, then transfer them to the serving dishes and serve immediately.

caramelized orange and pineapple

preparation time **10 mins**
cooking time **10 mins**
total time **20 mins** serves **4**

4 oranges
175 g/6 oz sugar
125 ml/4 fl oz water
1 small pineapple

one With a very sharp knife, remove the rind from 2 of the oranges and slice it into very fine strips. Place the rind in a saucepan of boiling water and simmer for 2 mins. Remove and drain well.

two Put the sugar and water into a saucepan and heat gently, swishing the pan constantly until the sugar is dissolved. Increase the heat and boil the syrup until it turns a golden brown. Take care not to overcook the caramel – if it gets too dark, carefully add 2 tablespoons of water. Stand back when adding the water as the caramel spits. Set aside when ready.

three To peel the oranges, cut a slice off the top and bottom of each one, then place the orange on one of these cut sides and take a knife around the side of the orange, cutting away the skin and pith. Cut across the orange into about 6–7 slices.

four To prepare the pineapple, top and tail it and slice away the skin from top to bottom. Make sure that you remove the 'eyes' close to the skin. Cut the pineapple into quarters and remove the core. Cut into slices.

five Make alternate layers of orange and pineapple in a heatproof dish. Sprinkle with the orange rind, pour over the caramel and leave to stand until required.

panettone pudding

preparation time **5 mins**
cooking time **25 mins**
total time **30 mins** serves **4**

50 g/2 oz butter
5 slices of panettone
a little apricot jam, for spreading
250 ml/8 fl oz milk
250 ml/8 fl oz double cream
2 eggs
1 egg yolk
50 g/2 oz brown sugar, plus extra for the crust

one Butter a 1.2 litre/2 pint ovenproof dish. Spread the panettone slices with the apricot jam and cut them into triangles or rectangles. Place in the buttered dish; try and arrange them in overlapping layers.

two Put the milk and cream into a saucepan and bring gently to the boil.

three Whisk together the eggs, egg yolk and sugar in a bowl until creamy and fluffy. Continue whisking and slowly add the hot milk and cream. When it is all combined, carefully pour it over the panettone; make sure that it is all covered by the custard mixture. Sprinkle with a little extra sugar to make a nice crunchy crust.

four Fill a roasting tin with boiling water, place the panettone pudding in the bain marie and bake in a preheated oven, 180°C (350°F), Gas Mark 4, for 25 mins or until the custard is set.

This dish is very good if prepared up to the cooking stage the night before and then kept in the refrigerator. This allows the panettone to soak up the custard.

lemon polenta syrup cake

preparation time **5 mins**
cooking time **25 mins**
total time **30 mins** serves **4–6**

175 g/6 oz butter
175 g/6 oz caster sugar
125 g/4 oz ground almonds
50 g/2 oz flaked almonds
½ teaspoon vanilla extract
2 large eggs
finely grated rind and juice of 1 lemon
75 g/3 oz polenta flour
½ teaspoon baking powder
single cream, to serve

SYRUP
grated rind and juice of 2 lemons
50 g/2 oz caster sugar
2 tablespoons of water

one Line a 15 cm/6 inch cake tin with baking parchment.

two Beat together the butter and sugar in a bowl until light and creamy. Add the ground and flaked almonds, vanilla extract and eggs and mix well. Add the lemon rind and juice, polenta and baking powder and mix well. Spoon into the prepared tin and bake in a preheated oven, 180°C (350°F), Gas Mark 4, for 25 mins.

three While the cake is cooking, make the syrup. Put the lemon rind and juice, caster sugar and water into a saucepan and heat through. Spoon over the cake as soon as it comes out of the oven. Allow the syrup to drizzle through. Serve the cake hot or cold with single cream.

almond soufflés

preparation time **10 mins**
cooking time **12 mins**
total time **22 mins** serves **4**

15 g/½ oz butter, plus extra for greasing
25 g/1 oz plain flour, plus extra for dusting
200 ml/7 fl oz milk
75 g/3 oz ground almonds
3 eggs, separated
25 g/1 oz caster sugar
75 ml/3 fl oz Amaretto di Saronno
4 macaroons, crushed
icing sugar, to decorate

one Butter 4 small soufflé dishes and dust with flour.

two Melt the butter in a small saucepan, add the flour and stir to a smooth paste. Slowly pour in the milk, stirring constantly, to make a smooth sauce. Add the ground almonds and egg yolks and mix well and rapidly. Do not leave the pan on the heat. Add the caster sugar and the Amaretto and mix well again.

three Quickly whisk the egg whites in a large bowl until stiff. Fold in the almond sauce, then quickly fold in the crushed macaroons.

four Divide the mixture between the prepared soufflé dishes and cook in a preheated oven, 220°C (425°F), Gas Mark 7, for 12 mins or until risen and golden. Dust with icing sugar and serve immediately.

These macaroons are delicious served with coffee. They can be stored in an airtight container for up to 10 days.

almond macaroons

preparation time **10 mins**
cooking time **15 mins**
total time **25 mins** makes approximately **16**

125 g/4 oz ground almonds
150 g/5 oz caster sugar
2 large egg whites
½ teaspoon almond extract

one Line 3 baking sheets with baking parchment.
two Mix the ground almonds and sugar together thoroughly. Whisk the egg whites and almond extract in a large bowl until stiff and glossy. Add the ground almond mixture to the egg whites and fold in until evenly blended.
three Using a small teaspoon, place spoonfuls of the mixture on the baking sheets leaving space between them so that they can expand slightly. Place the baking sheets in a preheated oven, 180°C (350°F), Gas Mark 4, and bake for 15 mins. The macaroons should be golden and slightly firm to the touch.
four Remove the macaroons from the oven and leave for 5 mins to cool and set. Lift them off the baking parchment with a thin palette knife and leave to cool completely.

baked peaches with almonds and honey

preparation time **5 mins**
cooking time **15 mins**
total time **20 mins** serves **4**

50 g/2 oz butter, plus extra for greasing
4 large ripe peaches, halved and stoned
50 g/2 oz flaked almonds
4 tablespoons clear honey
a little ground cinnamon
crème fraîche, to serve

one Butter a shallow baking dish large enough to take 8 peach halves.
two Place the peaches in the baking dish, skin side down. Dot with butter, then sprinkle with the almonds, drizzle with the honey and dust with cinnamon.
three Bake the peaches at the top of a preheated oven, 200°C (400°F), Gas Mark 6, for 10–15 mins. You want to get a little colour into the peaches and allow the almonds to lightly brown.
four Serve the peaches with the juices drizzled over and topped with a spoonful of crème fraîche.

almond brittle

preparation time **5 mins**
cooking time **10 mins**
total time **15 mins** serves **8**

250 g/8 oz blanched almonds
250 g/8 oz sugar

one Line a baking tray with baking
parchment.
two Put the almonds on a grill pan and place
under a preheated grill until lightly brown.
Allow to cool a little, then roughly chop.
three Heat a nonstick frying pan over a
moderate heat, add the sugar and allow to
melt into caramel. Take care that the heat is
not too high or the caramel will burn and
have a very bitter taste. Add the almonds
and mix in, then pour the almond brittle into
the prepared baking tray.
four Leave the almond brittle to cool, then
break it into small pieces.

Serve this almond brittle with ice cream or
good strong coffee. Store it in an airtight
container.

poached pears with honey and cinnamon

preparation time **5 mins**
cooking time **20 mins**
total time **25 mins** serves **4**

rind and juice of 1 lemon
450 ml/¾ pint red wine
150 ml/5 fl oz water
5 tablespoons clear honey
1 mace blade
1 cinnamon stick
6 cloves
4 ripe pears, peeled
thick yogurt, to serve

one Put the lemon rind and juice, wine,
water, honey, mace, cinnamon and cloves
into a saucepan and bring to a gentle boil.
two Add the pears and simmer for 10 mins or
until they are soft, turning them occasionally.
three Remove the pears with a slotted
spoon and set aside. Transfer the liquid to
a saucepan with a larger surface area. Place
the pan over a high heat and boil the liquid
rapidly to make a rich, thick, sticky syrup.
Spoon the syrup over the pears and serve
with thick yogurt.

Serve the chocolate risotto in coffee cups for an Italian flavour. Use a good-quality dark chocolate with a high percentage of cocoa butter – at least 70%.

chocolate risotto

preparation time **5 mins**
cooking time **20 mins**
total time **25 mins** serves **4**

600 ml/1 pint milk
25 g/1 oz sugar
50 g/2 oz butter
125 g/4 oz arborio or carnaroli rice
50 g/2 oz hazelnuts, toasted and chopped
50 g/2 oz sultanas
125 g/4 oz good-quality dark chocolate, grated
splash of brandy (optional)
grated chocolate, to decorate

one Put the milk and sugar into a saucepan and heat to simmering point.
two Melt the butter in a heavy-based saucepan, add the rice and stir well to coat the grains.
three Add a ladleful of hot milk and stir well. When the rice has absorbed the milk, add another ladleful. Continue to add the milk in stages and stir until it is all absorbed. The rice should be slightly *al dente* and with a creamy sauce.
four Finally, add the hazelnuts, sultanas and grated chocolate and mix quickly. Serve decorated with a little grated chocolate. Try not to overmix the chocolate as the marbled effect looks good. For a special treat, add a splash of brandy just before decorating and serving the risotto.

sweet risotto

preparation time **5 mins**
cooking time **20 mins**
total time **25 mins** serves **4**

600 ml/1 pint milk
25 g/1 oz sugar
½ teaspoon vanilla extract
50 g/2 oz butter
finely grated rind of 1 lemon
125 g/4 oz arborio or carnaroli rice
50 g/2 oz raisins
50 g/2 oz toasted flaked almonds
3 tablespoons honey

one Put the milk, sugar and vanilla extract into a saucepan and heat to simmering point, then turn off the heat.
two Melt the butter in a heavy-based saucepan, add the lemon rind and rice and mix well to coat the grains.
three Add the raisins and a ladleful of hot milk and stir well. When the rice has absorbed the milk, add another ladleful. Continue to add the milk in stages and stir until it is all absorbed. The rice should be slightly *al dente* and with a creamy sauce.
four Serve the risotto in individual dishes, sprinkled with toasted flaked almonds and drizzled with honey.

This unusual sweet risotto is not unlike a creamy rice pudding, but with more flavour.

Index

Acknowledgements

Executive Editor: Sarah Ford
Project Editor: Jessica Cowie
Executive Art Editor: Geoff Fennell
Designer: Sue Michniewicz

Photographer: David Loftus
Stylist: Wei Tang
Home Economist: Fran Warde
Production Controller: Ian Paton